SOME COMMONLY ASKED QUESTIONS NEW PARENTS HAVE THEIR FIRST WEEK AFTER ARRIVING ON PLANET PARENTHOOD . . .

MOM:

☀ Why can't I get around to taking a shower until after 5 P.M.?

☀ No one can make me actually go outside with this baby, can they?

☀ Will the visiting nurse come back and show me how to swaddle just one more time?

☀ How many calls can I make to my pediatrician before she sues me for harassment?

☀ What if I break the baby?

DAD:

☀ Why do phone company commercials make my wife cry?

☀ Why does the baby only sleep during the day?

☀ Why won't the car seat actually fit in the car?

☀ Wouldn't it be better for everyone involved if I just set up a cot at the office?

☀ What if I break the baby?

PLANET PARENTHOOD

Bringing Home Baby Without
Losing Your Mind

JULIE TILSNER

Bantam 🐝 Books

New York Toronto London Sydney Auckland

This edition contains the complete text
of the original trade paperback edition.
NOT ONE WORD HAS BEEN OMITTED.

PLANET PARENTHOOD

A Bantam Book
PUBLISHING HISTORY
Contemporary Books trade paperback edition published April 2000
Bantam mass market edition / August 2001

ISBN: 0-553-58363-8

Published simultaneously in the United States and Canada

Bantam books are published by Bantam Books, a division of Random
House, Inc. Its trademark, consisting of the words "Bantam Books" and
the portrayal of a rooster, is Registered in U.S. Patent and Trademark
Office and in other countries. Marca Registrada. Bantam Books, 1540
Broadway, New York, New York 10036.

PRINTED IN THE UNITED STATES OF AMERICA

OPM   10   9   8   7   6   5   4   3   2   1

To **TISH** and **HERB**,

the original parents,

who taught me everything I know.

And to **L. L. LINDA**,

mother extraordinaire.

CONTENTS

Preface

GOT SLEEP?

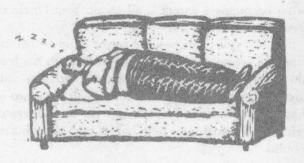

"If people really knew what they were in for once they had kids, they'd never have them."

—ANONYMOUS

So you're going to have a baby soon, huh? Congratulations.

Heh. I don't even know you and already I have the smirk on my face. You know the one—the bemused look all parents flash at parents-to-be. *That* one. The one that implies you simply don't know what you're in for, even though your nursery is finished and you've got enough frozen dinners stockpiled to last the first month.

I can't help it. No actual parent can help it. We simply know too much.

You bright-eyed parents-to-be never see the connection between having a baby and becoming a parent. You think you do. You buy all the stuff and read all the books. You carve out a little nursery in the extra room or the laundry nook and decorate it with lots of stuffed animals and pastel-colored bedding. But none of that is what becoming a parent is all about. Your Uncle Fred could do the same.

What you parents-to-be never seem to realize is that the change you're about to go through has less to do with the baby and everything to do with you. Babies are born preprogrammed for business. It's *you two* who bend and contort and morph into the servile creatures whose main goal is to help babies take their business public.

No doubt you've amassed an impressive library of how-to books on this very topic, hoping to glean something before you actually bring the kid home and the fun really starts. I'm sure you've got your What to Expect books and your updated version of Dr. Spock's classic. Well-meaning friends and relatives may even have given you books that try to address such hairy predicaments of parenting as *How to Play with Your Baby: 0–3 months* and *Identifying the Gifted Child*. There are thousands, probably millions, of these books seeking to answer any possible parenting question you may have, and probably a few nobody but the author cooked up.

This book isn't like any of those books.

The book you're clutching this very instant is about you. It's all about how you're going to change in the next twelve months—a full-on, Dolby stereo, Technicolor, 3-D transformation—from the normal person you are now, into the parent of somebody else. Parenthood is the kind of 180-degree flip that doesn't occur ever again in your life, not even after the births of subsequent children. It's the hardest life-change to get through unscathed, and when you've made it, you bear little resemblance to the person you were before. You won't think the same. You won't feel the same. Your politics will shift, probably to the right. And you certainly won't fit into any of your old clothes.

Let me put this as gently as I know how: parenthood is a state from which you never recover.

Here's as good an example as any: My husband, Luke, and I recently ran into a couple we met two years ago in our Lamaze class (and isn't *that* just a stomach-turning adult statement?). Tim and Elizabeth were an athletic, high-energy couple. Elizabeth found out she was pregnant in the midst of training for a triathlon. Tim hobbled into Lamaze classes with a leg broken on the slopes. They were the kind of couple you'd never find home on the weekends and who never got to bed before midnight. That was before they had their daughter. As we tried to get our toddlers to eat their pizza and not draw on the tables, we discussed topics that wouldn't have been on our radar three years ago: minivan models, preschool waiting lists, and the need for quiet neighbors. They were going to be moving soon, hopefully out of state, to where they could buy a home and not have to deal with people living above them.

"I actually had to go upstairs and ask the guys to keep it down because it was bedtime," said Tim.

"They're a bunch of single guys just out of college . . . you know . . ." He looked sheepish.

"And a couple of years ago you'd be up there having a beer with them, right?" I said.

"Yeah," he laughed. "Jeez, I never even *heard* them until two years ago."

We all laughed.

You have to laugh.

Which brings us to what kind of book this is, and what kind of book this is not. This is a humor book, or at least that's what it aspires to be. It's meant to cast a gimlet eye at the wacky transformations you'll go through in your first year as parents, and to do it in a lighthearted manner. Not in the laughing mood? There are plenty of scary, serious books on child raising out there on the market written with people like you in mind. All I'm going to say is I hope you find your sense of humor again and soon. You're going to need lots of it in the years to come.

What this is not is a book of advice on child raising. Sure, I offer up a few opinions of my own, but hey, it's my book. The only expertise I hold over you is that I've maybe been on Planet Parenthood for a few years longer, and as such I'm getting less sleep and am more inclined to get snippy with experts. If you want a solid medical degree behind your advice, best to consult Spock, Leach, Brazelton, or any number of expert voices out there, or ask that pediatrician you spent three months finding.

Stop worrying. You're going to be fine. And you're going to love being a parent, trust me. You're just not going to recognize yourself this time next year. Once you become a parent, you can't ever go back to the other side. But you're not going to want to, anyway. At least you'll be in good company.

Let me be the first to welcome you, then, to Planet Parenthood.

Introduction

THE CRAWLING ZONE

> "You can judge
> your parents until
> you become a
> parent yourself."
>
> —ANONYMOUS

INTO THE POOP

Parenthood ain't for sissies. There's a long and ugly list of initiation rites you have to suffer through, including but not limited to: sleepless nights, near-miss catastrophes, perplexing noises, ruined furniture, etc. etc. It takes twelve full months' worth of this kind of abuse before you can rightfully earn your citizenship on Planet Parenthood. Surviving childbirth is just the beginning, merely your invitation ticket. The really hard part hasn't even started yet. But of course you allegedly know this already.

And so, as someone who took up residence on Planet Parenthood only a few short years ago and understands what effect extreme sleep deprivation has on your ability to absorb printed information, I've tried to break this book down into easy-to-digest nuggets. Don't worry about retaining any of the knowledge contained herein. No test will jump out at you at the end. You wouldn't be able to pass it if it did, anyway.

Please note the glossary of **Useful Terms** near the beginning of each chapter. These will help you understand the language on Planet Parenthood, the distinct patois that marks you as an insider to other parents, even without the baby on your person.

We start at ground zero—Week One, or as I call it, **Boot Camp, Baby**. This is your trial by fire, the week that separates forever the mice from the men, and too much of the time, the men from the moms. We look at several unique and never-to-be-repeated (thank God) phenomena that take place during the first seven days of life with your baby. Yes, the Poop List is included.

From the second week through three months you're **Adapting to Your New Life-Form**. The mute terror of the first week has passed, and you're starting to see what you're in for and digging in for the long haul. These are the sleepless weeks, the adjustment period when you dramatically downsize each of your prechild parenting ideals to something more realistic (usually whatever reaps you ten more minutes of sleep). You're just beginning to think of yourself as a parent, even as you realize that giant consumer-goods companies have viewed you as such for months now.

♡ ♡ ♡ ♡ ♡ ♡ ♡ ♡ ♡ ♡ ♡ ♡ ♡ ♡ ♡ ♡ ♡ ♡

A NOTE ON LANGUAGE

For the record, I'm behind loving parents in any incarnation—single parents, gay parents, mixed-race parents, unmarried parents, whatever. Single moms especially. If it were up to me you'd all get medals for unusual heroism, as well as state-subsidized houseboys.

But within this book I often rely on such quaint words as <u>spouse</u> and <u>husband/wife</u> only because the narrative flow demands it. If I tried to be PC and include every coupling possible in this era, I wouldn't be able to write a sentence. What happens to you when you become a parent is pretty universal, and it hardly matters what incarnation your new family takes. So keep calm—I am talking to *you.*

♡ ♡ ♡ ♡ ♡ ♡ ♡ ♡ ♡ ♡ ♡ ♡ ♡ ♡ ♡ ♡ ♡ ♡

I call the period from between three months and six months **Adventures in Matrimony** because during this time the baby has settled down enough to allow you to examine the remains of your marriage. What happened to that adventurous, well-dressed guy you married? Where did that spontaneous, willowy girl go? Exactly when did you turn into your parents, anyway? And when, if ever, can you expect to turn back into yourselves? (Here's a hint: *Never!*) This chapter also offers tips on explaining yourselves to your single or child-free friends, or when that fails, finding and keeping a whole new circle of cronies—new-parent friends.

The Kodak Months—the period between six and eight months—are thus called because now you morph once again into another kind of parent—a *preening* parent. Babies at this age are most likely to be tapped for Baby Gap commercials. They're chubby and bubbling, and jolly as hell, slaying themselves with their own jokes. You're held in their thrall, and indeed you're so convinced you have the one authentic Wonder Baby in the universe that even other parents go out of their way to avoid you. We discuss the pleasures of feeding and forward mobility as well.

It's when you get that feeling of **Approaching Oneness**—during that blissful period from eight to twelve months—that you're inclined to get cocky—to think you've just about put this parenting thing to bed, so to speak. You haven't. Your life is about to be made much more complicated because now what you're dealing with is not so much a cute little baby as a mobile unit with a death wish. I detail what's going to happen to your home, your nerves, and your future, since if you're planning on doing the 2.5 kid thing, you'd better start thinking about planting the next one pretty soon.

So. Sound like a book you can use? Of course it does. You could use a laugh right about now.

You may notice a refreshing lack of "expert" opinions (besides my own) in this book. That's not to say that I don't value the opinions of experts, only that you've probably already got a stack of experts on your nightstand at this late date, and you certainly don't need me confusing you further. This is the era of parenting "by the book," and it's my uniquely nonexpert opinion that there are too many experts out there offering up often conflicting and contradictory advice to the terrified new parent. Why is that? I think it has something to do with the disintegration of the extended family. Mom and Grandma used to be the experts, but few people live near family anymore. Even if they do, they don't see any M.D. or Ph.D. behind Mom and Grandma's names and so feel they can't be qualified to weigh in on matters newborn. This is laughable, since if you're sitting here reading this, Mom must have done something right.

Parenting isn't rocket science. It involves a certain amount of practical know-how and lots of intuition and gut instinct. People have been doing it since people have been, um . . . *doing* it. Trouble is, in twenty-first-century America, intuition and gut instincts make people twitch. We like the hard facts, thank you ma'am, and we generally like things orderly and well-laid out, ideally with a clear set of instructions and a money-back guarantee. You will notice that babies don't come with any spec sheets, much less a warranty. They introduce a very scary wildcard into our whole sense of order, and from the moment they arrive they force everything around them to bend to their will. In this respect, you can see the wisdom in having children when you're too young and dumb to worry about any of this. But if you're not that young and dumb, chances are you're depending on the experts.

As far as experts go, I'm a Spock gal myself. It was Dr. Benjamin Spock who first enjoined new parents: "Relax. You know more than you think you do." He's right. You do. And when baby comes home for good, just keep calm and use your common sense and everybody will be happier. I'm not at all suggesting you don't need a few books by the experts lying around the house. On the contrary, they're handy when you need to look up what to do for ear infections at 3 A.M. But any more than that and you're just using up valuable bookshelf space, not to mention asking for it in an earthquake.

Historical Hysteria

"Babies don't come with instruction manuals," goes the old chestnut. At least mine didn't, so it must be true. Fortunately, there's never been any dearth of information or opinions on how to raise baby. Unfortunately, that information contradicts itself depending on which expert is doling it out. It also tends to change every generation.

In the 1930s, for example, the experts deemed that it was of the utmost importance that baby be kept on a feeding schedule so strict you could run a railroad on it. There was no gospel on breast feeding. Indeed, doctors told new mothers to get baby used to a bottle within the first month, so he would learn how to suck properly and get other important nutrients, such as watered-down orange juice. It was important for baby to finish his serving in one sitting so he would gain weight in a steady manner. Bottles were made of glass, of course, and nobody thought a thing about propping one up for baby to drink from while Mother left the room. Lots of cribs were made with detachable "arms" for just this purpose.

New mothers were encouraged to make their babies as independent as possible as fast as possible. Articles and books advised new mothers to start toilet training as early as four or five months, or as soon as baby could hold his head upright and sit supported on a potty Mother held in her lap. It was a scandalous reflection on your mothering skills if your child was still in diapers at age two. The baby book of the day was *Psychological Care of Infant and Child*, by Dr. John B. Watson. First published in 1928, it set the tone for mothering a generation: "Mothers just don't know when they kiss their children and pick them up and rock them, caress them, jiggle them upon their knee, that they are building up a human totally unable to cope with the world it must later live in."

By the '50s and '60s, the kinder, gentler Dr. Spock had replaced Dr. Watson on the nightstands of most new mothers, who now at least could pick up their crying babies in public without guilt. Breast feeding had fallen almost completely out of favor with the advent of the new scientific formulas that were supposed to be much healthier for baby, making her plumper, happier, and less prone to ear infections. When did you start introducing solid food to your baby? Why, at around three weeks of course. Get her going with a little strained meat or rice cereal mixed with cow's milk. Car seats were more an issue of style than substance, and if you had one at all it was a simple aluminum seat that slung over the back of the car seat. Granted, it was harder to total a car back then. And fathers were not expected to have anything to do with a new baby. That was exclusively the mother's job.

In the 1970s, the ideal way to raise children was without gender, racial, or sexual biases. Given the headlines thirty years later, you can see how successful that experiment's been.

These days we have our own set of rules and ideals for raising the better baby, and we of course act like these are written in stone. You've probably spent the last nine months reading everything you could get your hands on regarding the ins and outs of baby care. You've signed up for Lamaze and "Caring for Your Newborn" classes at your local hospital. You may even have thrown in a little Red Cross training, just in case. You may have hired a doula, a woman who will be at the birth with you to chant and rub your belly. You and your mate may have toured the maternity wings of various hospitals in your area, and, if you have really good insurance, you may try to reserve a "birthing suite" that resembles a hotel room more than anything else. Unlike in your own mother's day, Dad can be there to watch the birth and cut the umbilical cord or faint or whatever else he's inclined to do.

Also unlike your mother and grandmother, unless there are complications, you'll be out of the hospital within twenty-four hours of giving birth, since that's all your HMO will pay for. They'll wheel you into the lobby to check out, but they won't let you out the door until you show them your regulation car seat, which by law you're required to have now that you're a parent.

Once home with baby, you might get a visiting nurse sent out to check up on you, or a lactation consultant to train you on breast feeding. She'll also brief you on a number of new baby rules of the day, which you probably already know better than she does. For example, you know that you NEVER put baby down to sleep on his stomach, since that is thought to increase the chances of sudden infant death syndrome, or SIDS, an acronym you can barely utter without feeling nauseous—and which probably contributed to your buying one of those audio/video devices to attach to the crib so you can stare at your newborn's breathing for the first couple of months, as well as a $45 foam rubber crib prop to keep baby from inadvertently rolling over onto his stomach while sleeping.

You will at least try to exclusively breast feed for the first year, because you've been promised that breast-fed babies are bigger, have higher IQs, fewer ear infections, and are more bonded to their mothers than bottle-fed babies—the exact opposite of what they told new moms in the '50s and '60s. You will at least try to do the ecologically right thing and give cloth diapers a go. You have many pamphlets warning you never to give baby honey, or anything with honey in it, because of certain bacterial threats inherent in the stuff. And there probably isn't a bottle of those tiny pink St. Joseph's children's aspirins you remember from your own childhood in your medicine cabinet because now the experts tell us aspirin could possibly lead to the rare Reye's syndrome. Absolutely NO cow's milk before baby's first year, either—it might lead to infections, or low iron in the blood, or, heaven forbid, allergies! You've thrown out all the plastic teethers and other toys well-meaning relatives have given you because you've read that the *diisononyl phthalate* present in soft vinyl toys can cause liver and kidney damage. You think playpens and pacifiers are unacceptable crutches, and you vow to never use either. You make everyone who picks up your baby wash his hands first.

Believe me, your mother and her friends are screaming with laughter at you two behind your back.

And all this expert advice will change again. That newborn you have in your arms, snuggled in her hypoallergenic receiving blanket and listening to Mozart selections carefully selected to enrich her developing mind, will regard these practices as barbaric when she has her own children in twenty or thirty years' time. And it will be your turn to laugh.

PAGING DR. SPOCK

Another reason I favor Dr. Spock: not only is he a calm, reasonable voice in a growing sea of hysteria, but it was he who tried to point out to the masses that something in our culture is seriously amiss when the accumulation of money and the stuff money buys take on greater importance than the rearing of children.

Maybe this isn't an original thought, but there's a lot of personal sacrifice involved in this parenting gig. At least one of you, and ideally both of you, are going to have to give up a few things in order to raise this baby of yours—*and that's a good thing!* Contrary to modern American thinking, there is no job more important than launching the next generation. Putting somebody else's needs above your own creates character, strength, and maturity. That may be a terrifically passé thought, but it's the truth. You may be putting in your eighty-hour weeks so you can buy your child more of everything, but in the end, the child would rather have you. America talks a good game about "Family Values," but everything about its commercial, social, political, and media norms suggests otherwise. In the end, those of us on Planet Parenthood have to help ourselves.

Are you ready? Of course not, but it's time to get started. You've got a lot of changing to do, and I'm not just talking about diapers. Hopefully this book will help you keep the proper perspective as you change from the normal person you are now into a parent. You can fight this change, and triple your stress, or you can go with the flow.

Believe me, resistance is futile. Join us.

Chapter 1

BOOT CAMP, BABY

(Week 1)

*"It sometimes happens,
even in the best families, that
a baby is born. This is not
necessarily cause for alarm.
The important thing is to
keep your wits about you
and borrow some money."*
— ELINOR GOULDING SMITH

Hey, welcome home! Cute little baby you've got there (and I emphasize little). But you've got everything ready, your nursery (or your bassinet by the bed), your supply of baby clothes and diapers. The pediatrician's twenty-four-hour emergency hot line tacked to the wall in big black letters so you can read it no matter how little sleep you've gotten. Thirty-five receiving blankets at the ready, sent by every well-meaning friend or relative who had to buy you something. Baby dishes and cups and swings and gadgets you won't even look at for another six months. You've got nothing to worry about. You're set.

♡ ♡ ♡ ♡ ♡ ♡ ♡ ♡ ♡ ♡ ♡ ♡ ♡ ♡ ♡ ♡ ♡

USEFUL TERMS

Before now, the patois of parenthood bounced off your nonparent Teflon coating. You didn't need to know anything about varicose veins before you were pregnant, and you were blissfully ignorant of stroller brands and day care costs before now as well. No longer. Now that you're parents, you've got to learn how to talk the talk.

Parent shoptalk is mostly euphemism. Nobody will ever come right out and say what he means, relying instead on several layers of padding to shield you from reality. Other terms are pretty straightforward ... they're just completely meaningless to the average nonparent. Here are some of the basic new terms and euphemisms you can expect to come across in your new life as a parent.

APGAR TEST A test developed to describe your baby's condition at birth on a scale of 1 to 10, using color, cry, and movement as a barometer. No more, no less. But of course parents still tell you when their baby scored a 10.

BM Bowel Movement. Poop to you and me, or insert your own personal descriptive noun here.

FONTANEL That scary soft spot on baby's head where the skull hasn't closed yet. Don't worry, it will go away soon.

♡ ♡ ♡ ♡ ♡ ♡ ♡ ♡ ♡ ♡ ♡ ♡ ♡ ♡ ♡ ♡ ♡

♡ ♡ ♡ ♡ ♡ ♡ ♡ ♡ ♡ ♡ ♡ ♡ ♡ ♡ ♡ ♡ ♡ ♡

LAYETTE A color-coordinated newborn outfit set. Something a lot of the older women in your family will buy for you. Your newborn won't notice at all except to spit up all over it.

MOSES BASKET A soft, pillow-lined basket for your newborn to sleep in. Much smaller than a bassinet, and much more chichi than the version Moses went down the river on. You'll pay a lot more for yours than Moses' mom did for his.

NIPPLE CONFUSION What happens when baby tries both a bottle nipple and a real nipple and, apparently, gets the two confused. Lactation enthusiasts consider this a dread condition that will thwart your effort to breast feed.

ONESIE A one-piece baby outfit with snaps on the bottom. For diaper changing, you novice!

RECEIVING BLANKETS Soft, pastel-colored baby blankets that you will swaddle baby in during the early days and use for burp cloths very soon after that. This is fine, since you have hundreds of them.

♡ ♡ ♡ ♡ ♡ ♡ ♡ ♡ ♡ ♡ ♡ ♡ ♡ ♡ ♡ ♡ ♡ ♡

Then why are you looking so scared?

This is it, guys. This is what you worried about from the first time you ever had sex right on through those Lamaze classes. This is your first week of parenthood—

or as many more-seasoned moms and dads refer to it, Boot Camp Time. This is where all your reading, all those baby first-aid classes, all that time spent scouring the Internet for more information leaves you high and dry. It was nothing but primer, you'll soon be realizing. Background information. A good base. Now that you've actually got your baby in hand, the all-important hands-on experience starts.

Yes, I know how you feel. I distantly remember my first week as a mom: my glowing parents doting over their new grandchild, changing a few diapers, stocking our larder with food and then deserting us; the mysteries of breast feeding still undeciphered; the visiting nurse; rampaging hormones.

One emotion surpassed all others, however. Abject, stomach-turning terror. I remember the very first night after my parents left. Luke and I sat on the floor staring at each other, with every one of our parenting books open and cross-referenced as Annie lay peacefully sleeping in her bassinet. Around 10 P.M., when we had begun to think that maybe everyone had been exaggerating about the amount of sleep we could expect in the first three months, Annie began to cry, softly at first, and then building into a prolonged wail. Then she wouldn't go on the breast. Then the neighbors knocked. By the third night of this, my husband made the profound observation that the most difficult thing to come to terms with was that we couldn't just put her back in the box when we'd had enough. This was forever. We were parents. Nobody else was going to deal with it. We would not be hitting the snooze bar on our alarm clock for at least a decade.

You've heard of sink or swim? Better start kicking those legs.

YOUR PARENTS' REVENGE

Remember back when you were a surly teenager, vexing your parents by dying your hair unnatural colors or getting yourself kicked out of school? Remember how your parents would wag a weary finger at you and say some variation on the following: "Just wait until you have kids"? You, of course, would sneer and ignore them because you were not planning on being the suburban, breeding type. You were going to be a rock star. Or a poet. Or a famous anarchist. Naturally, you would not ever be having kids.

Now that you're more evolved, you may have forgotten episodes like these. But rest assured, your parents have not.

Sure, your folks are probably thrilled with the latest addition to the family, and are no doubt secretly amazed that any kid of theirs grew up to take on the responsibility of a child. But beneath these shiny happy feelings lurks something darker. It's the need for some small measure of revenge. No mere human can resist the urge to finally laugh and say "I told you so." Not even your sainted mother is immune to this urge.

Now that you've just had your first child, now that you're feeling more vulnerable than you can ever remember feeling, and now that you're experiencing emotions we don't have words for, your parents are going to let you have it. Don't think for a moment that they're not watching you, gleefully thinking to themselves, *At last! Revenge is mine!* Mom and Dad are old hands at this parenting stuff. They did it themselves and were probably ten years younger than you are now when they did. They know what's coming, and you and your mate only *think* you do. You're not fooling them, either. They know you've never changed a diaper before today.

The first small act of revenge on you from your parents comes early. It hinges on one small fact that you, in your hormonal stupor, may have overlooked until now:

When the crying gets too loud, your parents can leave.

You can't.

You're the parents now. Your own parents have waited for this moment for many years. Indeed, they may even have calculated the cruelest moment at which to look at their watches and slip out the door (usually when the baby wakes up for the night).

Contrary to popular belief, parenthood doesn't start when you give birth, although it sure as hell feels like it. Nor does it officially start in the hospital, where a group of skilled professionals are mopping your brow and bringing you food. Even if you are "rooming in," that is, spending your first precious night after birth with baby instead of parceling it out to the nursery, you've still got a professional nurse coming around every few hours to make sure your gross ineptitude hasn't killed it.

♡ ♡ ♡ ♡ ♡ ♡ ♡ ♡ ♡ ♡ ♡ ♡ ♡ ♡ ♡ ♡ ♡

ASSORTED FIRST-WEEK QUESTIONS

MOM:

☼ Why can't I get around to taking a shower until after 5 p.m.?

☼ No one can make me actually go outside with this baby, can they?

☼ Will the visiting nurse come back and show me how to swaddle just one more time?

☼ How many calls can I make to my pediatrician before she sues me for harassment?

☼ What if I break the baby?

DAD:

☼ Why do phone company commercials make my wife cry?

☼ Why does the baby only sleep during the day?

☼ Why won't the car seat actually fit in the car?

☼ Wouldn't it be better for everyone involved if I just set up a cot at the office?

☼ What if I break the baby?

♡ ♡ ♡ ♡ ♡ ♡ ♡ ♡ ♡ ♡ ♡ ♡ ♡ ♡ ♡ ♡ ♡

Parenting doesn't really start at home, either, because since this is your first baby, you're probably still
being, pardon the expression, pampered. There's nothing new grandparents like better than to spend a little
time with you just after the arrival of your baby.
Grandma is only too happy to take over the daytime
care of the little one, showing you essentials like how
to make the diapers fit and how to actually hold the
thing. Grandpas are generally willing to do manly
things, such as buy you groceries for a couple of weeks,
tune your car, assemble the bouncy seat. All of this
gives you and your mate a grace period, and I suggest
you use it to catch up on your sleep. Grandparents
have been known to linger for weeks on end, giving
you a very false sense that maybe this baby thing isn't
as bad as people made it out to be. Be forewarned that
all babies behave better when being manhandled by
Grandma. Maybe they sense that, for a few days anyway, they're in competent hands. In coming months,
your baby will always quiet down in Grandma's arms,
play quietly, perform various tricks of dexterity and
verbiage, and of course eat all manner of things he
won't eat for you. This does nothing for your self-
esteem. But I'm getting ahead of myself.

Parenthood officially begins the moment all older,
wiser, and more experienced friends and relatives leave
you, your mate, and the new baby to your own devices.
At the designated time, your parents will look over their
shoulders and smile, with barely any indication of malice,
as they move their luggage to the car. Indeed, the mirth in

their eyes is directly proportional to the size of that rock in your stomach. Feel that weight crashing down on your shoulders like a two-ton cartoon barbell? That's parent-hood, baby. And don't your parents know it!

"Having a baby is like suddenly getting the world's worst roommate, like having Janis Joplin with a bad hangover and PMS come to stay with you."
—ANNE LAMOTT

Of course, these days, many couples make a big deal about wanting to spend the first week *alone* with their baby, without visitors or well-wishers. They want to spend some quiet time as a new family, getting to know each other, bonding.

Please take it from a seasoned parent: this is ca-ca.

A newborn baby does four things: it sleeps, it eats, it cries, it poops. You're only "bonding" with her inas-much as you're holding her, suckling her, and keeping her warm. You and she are not exchanging deep, lov-ing looks. For the first few weeks she is looking at something vaguely over your left shoulder, not at you. (Actually, when she can focus at all after a few weeks, she can see about eight inches in front of her—about the distance from your arms to your nipple, which is frankly all she cares about.) There's a theory that a baby isn't even fully cooked until three or four months, and that the only reason it's been born before then is because otherwise the human head gets too big to birth (there's evolution for you). In these terms, you have a month or so to play with before you have to get out the flash cards. Besides, as mentioned above, once everyone leaves, you'll have the next eighteen years to bond.

Secondly, the standard definition of family includes the newborn as well as everyone else who's been hanging around up until now, and that includes your own parents, sisters, brothers, and in-laws. Letting them help out in the first week only helps you in the long run. They'll all leave you alone sooner or later (you can count on that much), and in the meantime, your laundry is getting done and somebody else is doing the grocery shopping. Take all the help you can get in this first week, for God's sake, and use this time wisely to stock up on sleep.

FUN WITH HORMONES

Deciding to have a baby is a big enough deal. Birthing that baby (or watching it birthed) is another trauma entirely. But now that you've brought your baby home, you're dimly aware that the next couple of weeks are going to be taxing. Sleep deprivation. Constant pressure to keep the baby alive and breathing. Painful stitches in unlikely places. On top of all of this, at least one of you is experiencing hormone hell.

Yes, you read about postpartum depression, didn't

you? But did any of those books accurately describe what childbirth was like? No, they did not, thank you. So what you understand to be postpartum depression may not be what you actually get. Just rest assured that you'll get something. The hormones are coming to get you, and there's no escape.

You remember hormones. They're what made adolescence so frustrating and sticky. They also got you through pregnancy, putting you on autopilot so that you didn't mind eating mountains of mashed potatoes and falling asleep at six every night. They're what kept you from going insane at the mere idea of somebody else growing inside of you.

Now those pregnancy hormones are getting the idea that they're no longer needed—but in their haste to get out the door they're crashing into all the "mommy" hormones on the way in. The result is hormonal soup. Or as the books call it, the Baby Blues. It's a completely normal and natural phenomenon that nevertheless throws most women a curveball in the first few weeks after giving birth.

Here are some everyday situations that will overwhelm you in the first week of parenthood, thanks to hormonal soup:

☀ A telemarketer calls. He asks you to consider switching your long distance company to his, and offers you a special bonus! You can't decide. Start to cry.

☀ Your husband runs to the store to buy more formula. Worry he'll never come back, abandoning you and your tiny new baby. Start to cry.

☀ A TV commercial comes on. It's for Save the Children. For $20 a month, you can save a starving child in Africa. Decide to write check for $40 but can't find pen. Can't cope, start to cry.

☀ It's late afternoon. Sunlight streams through the curtains and into your sleeping baby's bassinet. Start to cry.

☀ It's midevening. Baby wakes up for the night. Remember wistfully what it was like to experience REM sleep. Start to cry. (Dad may join in on this one.)

This state of mind alarms a lot of women, most of whom had no problem hanging up on people or writing checks until recently. But rest assured, you're not alone. Millions of new mothers spend the first week after childbirth alternately crying for no discernible reason, loving their babies beyond reason, and feeling like they've just ruined their lives forever. Because of postpartum hormones, all complex thought processes come to a screaming halt, and there is very little in the way of decision making or logic that you're able to do. If you want to look at this as "depression," go right ahead. But it's nicer to simply view it as a nice little thirty-day holiday for your brain. If you dislike crying for no reason while all alone at home, consider joining a new mother group. There you can meet with other new moms and tell labor stories, and when everyone starts to weep while breast feeding, nobody will notice.

♡ ♡ ♡ ♡ ♡ ♡ ♡ ♡ ♡ ♡ ♡ ♡ ♡ ♡ ♡ ♡ ♡ ♡

WHAT YOU NEED AND WHAT YOU DON'T

What you really need in the first three months of your new life with baby are servants. A full-time English governess like the ones in all the Merchant Ivory films. And a live-in maid. And a cook with a special certificate in nutrition for lactating mothers. You would also be grateful for a driver, a masseur, and a personal assistant, thank you very much. But it's so hard to find good help these days, and besides, who's got a west wing to house them in anymore? Aside from Demi Moore and Madonna, I mean.

The rest of us should be happy that the hospital bill won't come for another few months. Beyond that, there isn't much you actually need for baby's arrival on the scene, despite what the parenting books and magazines would have you believe.

Chances are, the minute you announced your pregnancy it was as if the universe opened up and began to rain baby products upon your household anyway. If

♡ ♡ ♡ ♡ ♡ ♡ ♡ ♡ ♡ ♡ ♡ ♡ ♡ ♡ ♡ ♡ ♡ ♡

♡ ♡ ♡ ♡ ♡ ♡ ♡ ♡ ♡ ♡ ♡ ♡ ♡ ♡ ♡ ♡ ♡ ♡

your girlfriends didn't throw you a shower or three, then your mother or mother-in-law whipped out her platinum card to celebrate the impending newest member of the family. Or else the older ladies at work chipped in to buy you items you'd never known existed before this.

The truth of things is this: although decorating your nursery was a labor of love on your part, your newborn is completely oblivious to the fact that the wallpaper borders match the blanket set in the crib. She has no comment on the hand-stenciled bunnies gracing the walls of her nursery, nor the tasteful array of expensive stuffed animals on the new solid-oak nursery wardrobe. It's hard for new parents—particularly <u>American</u> new parents who've been conditioned since birth to spend money—to realize that a newborn can be just as happy wrapped in soft, clean towels in a shoebox as in a $5,000 Gucci crib.

Here's what you really, really need when you find a newborn in the house:

☀ A clean, warm place for her to sleep
☀ A car seat—it's the law
☀ A few soft receiving blankets to swaddle her in
☀ Newborn-size diapers
☀ Several sleepers or onesies
☀ Ok, ok, go ahead and buy some rattle toys because you can't help yourself

♡ ♡ ♡ ♡ ♡ ♡ ♡ ♡ ♡ ♡ ♡ ♡ ♡ ♡ ♡ ♡ ♡ ♡

♡ ♡ ♡ ♡ ♡ ♡ ♡ ♡ ♡ ♡ ♡ ♡ ♡ ♡ ♡ ♡ ♡ ♡

☼ Here are a few items now on the market that you do *not* need:

☼ A camcorder that videotapes your baby as she sleeps while you watch her on a monitor in the kitchen

☼ Aromatherapy kit for your baby

☼ Stuffed animals that play sounds of the womb, purportedly to comfort your baby into slumber (or make you think your washing machine in the basement is broken)

☼ Baby utensils that measure the temperature of her food (you won't even be using utensils for another year. And what ever happened to blowing on hot food?)

☼ A high-tech cradle that rocks automatically depending on where baby is in her REM sleep

♡ ♡ ♡ ♡ ♡ ♡ ♡ ♡ ♡ ♡ ♡ ♡ ♡ ♡ ♡ ♡ ♡ ♡

Besides, there's an upside to this state of mind. Nature didn't turn you into a weepy, indecisive idiot just for laughs, you know. You'll emerge from your first weeks as a new mother with New Mother powers. Remember all the magic your mom could do? Those little triangle sandwiches with the crusts cut off? Hormones did that. Some other amazing feats you'll be able to perform include:

☼ Hearing your own baby's cry out of a roomful of crying babies. Good for day care situations.

☀ Smelling your baby's poop from three blocks down the street.

☀ Staring down rottweilers, strange old ladies who want to pinch your baby's cheeks, and stroller salesmen.

☀ Reading your baby's mind (this irritates many new dads, who don't get any new hormones to play with).

☀ Assembling *anything*.

The good news is postpartum depression doesn't last very long. One or two weeks usually, just long enough for severe sleep deprivation to kick in and take over the job of keeping both new parents blissfully stupefied. Sleep deprivation will get you through the next three months, just long enough for the final hormonal joke to rear its ugly head.

Three months is around the time women begin to look back on childbearing as an experience that wasn't so bad after all. "Intense" is the adjective most often heard in conjunction with memories of childbirth. Soon thereafter, you'll wake up one morning, fresh from, say, five whole hours of sleep, and think, *Hmm. I could use another newborn around the house*.

In the first weeks after childbirth, any thought of doing any of this ever again gives you the shakes. But hormones know this. So they wait a few months until the household has settled down a bit before they spring this last one on you. Cruel, yes, but how else would nature get you to get back in the ring and propagate the species? Fortunately, the man of the house is just snapping out of his sleep-deprivation stupor by this time and can squelch such foolishness promptly.

LACTATION NATION

Once upon a time, before man invented the plastic bottle, every woman who could breast feed her children did so. After all, that's why God gave us boobs, right? Women who couldn't breast feed, for whatever reason, either hightailed it to the nearest wet nurse or passed the kid over to a more milky relative. One rarely heard whines about cracked nipples or faulty breast pumps back in those days, since if you wanted to keep your child alive, you exercised the only option you had. Rubber nipples hadn't been invented yet.

But sometime in the '40s and '50s, breast feeding fell out of vogue among progressive circles. New, scientific formulas were being developed that were pushed as better, more sanitary, and more convenient for mother and baby, so several generations of us never knew the warmth of mother's milk. That right there, in certain circles these days, is tantamount to generational child abuse.

In the '70s, the breast came back in a big way (maybe it had something to do with all those burning bras?), and suddenly breast was best in every instance. The La Leche League published its classic *The Womanly Art of Breast Feeding*, and formula makers were boycotted. In the '80s or '90s, educated, professional moms took this to a new level, and we began to see "lactation centers" popping up in hospitals around the country, staffed by "certified lactation counselors." You might have met one of these ladies during your hospital stay.

Keep her number. Sometime in the first week, you will learn what it means to have your "milk come in." Hormones again—in some cases your breasts will grow four sizes before your very eyes as they fill with milk, ready to feed your newly hungry baby. Your husband's eyes may well be bugging out of his head by this point, but he won't be getting anywhere near you. These boobs are not the fun boobs he remembers from your preparenthood days. These boobs are for business.

Now that your breasts qualify you for a job on "Baywatch," you'll learn the cruel truth about breast feeding. As natural as it is, lots of babies don't get it right away. They can't get their mouths around the nipple (now the size of a dinner plate), and they wouldn't know what to do with it anyway. Neither do you, unless you grew up on a dairy farm (and I wish I were exaggerating). Begging your days-old infant to "Suck this!" rarely works, either.

Here, unfortunately, is where the lactation counselor comes in. In olden days, a new mother had a dozen womenfolk around to show her the ins and outs of breast feeding. But your mom probably fed you formula, so you've got to call the lactation counselor, sometimes also known (never to her face) as the Lactation Nazi.

This woman, whom you've never seen before, will have her hand on your breast within three minutes of her arrival. Somebody's got to show you how to "express milk," that is, milk yourself so that your boobs don't explode before baby can get to them. She'll also feel around for any clogged milk ducts (which can get infected and propel you into a whole new world of pain), and hopefully teach you how to tell the difference between a duct and, say, a tumor, especially if you tend to be hysterical about such things, like me.

After she has poked and prodded you, your lactation counselor will then grab your little newborn, force her mouth open, and unceremoniously "latch" her onto your giant breast. This is a horrifying thing to watch, since you're sure you're only going to smother the baby with your nipple (did I mention it now resembles a dinner plate?). She'll do this over and over again, explaining that since you can't reason with newborns, you have to teach them what's right by repeated efforts and rewards, along the Pavlov's dog model. After much effort on the counselor's part (and much wailing on yours), the baby might actually clue in and start to suck. That's when you're in for another amazing element of breast feeding—the "let down." Upon sensing your offspring's first feeble suck, your body—thanks to those hormones again—immediately opens the milk tap. Baby can then drink herself blind. This also means you won't wake up with a dry shirt until baby's eating something else. Be forewarned that from here on out, you are a walking drippy faucet. The mere sight of a baby can set you off. So can sex, hot showers, and particularly touching long-distance phone company commercials.

♡ ♡ ♡ ♡ ♡ ♡ ♡ ♡ ♡ ♡ ♡ ♡ ♡ ♡ ♡ ♡ ♡ ♡

CONVENTIONAL WISDOM THAT WILL NEVER MAKE SENSE

SLEEP WHEN THE BABY SLEEPS. Just when you're supposed to eat, shower, pay bills, do the laundry, do the dishes, make the bed, call the pediatrician, call Mom to cry, or pump more breast milk is never explained . . .

TAKE TIME OUT FOR JUST THE TWO OF YOU. As if you have any interest in sex in this first week (the very thought makes you faint). As if HE has any interest in sex, watching what you just went through. And as if either of you had any time at all, you wouldn't just take the opportunity to sleep for thirty-six hours straight . . .

EAT A HEALTHY, WELL-BALANCED MEAL TO KEEP UP YOUR BREAST MILK. Sure thing. But until the professional chef shows up at your door, you'll continue making do with breakfast cereal and canned soup.

KEEP THE LINES OF COMMUNICATION OPEN. Does that include grunting and the odd strangled sob?

ENJOY THIS PERIOD, IT'S OVER SO QUICKLY. Yeah, not soon enough . . .

♡ ♡ ♡ ♡ ♡ ♡ ♡ ♡ ♡ ♡ ♡ ♡ ♡ ♡ ♡ ♡ ♡ ♡

Breast feeding is not for the weak of heart or will. All the glowing La Leche literature never tells you about the horrifying realities. Assuming you sleep at all in the first week, you will wake up at dawn with your chest on fire, breasts the size of Pittsburgh, and a soaked T-shirt. You'll try to relieve yourself by getting baby to drink up, but newborns often haven't grasped the concept of "lunchtime." When baby does finally latch on, the pain can be fantastic. A lot of women swear that this pain goes away after the first month and then breast feeding actually becomes pleasurable, but until that time, the sensation more resembles what you imagine having the marrow sucked out of your bones might feel like.

For the first time in your life, your breasts have a life of their own. They self-regulate, generating as much or as little milk as your baby takes in a feeding. They turn on and off by themselves. They work everything you put into your mouth into little milk-based snacks for baby. They also clog up and get infected and leak at embarrassing moments, and generally become both your obsession and the bane of your existence.

And that's just the physical part. You should see the equipment. There are nursing bras that cost $40 a pop and look like garden-party hats. There are breast pumps that range from the handheld to the $300 "hospital-quality" versions with the horsepower of emergency backup generators. There is even a version cleverly disguised as a briefcase that you can take to work with you. It hooks up to both breasts at once, so you can "express" your baby's dinner bottle before the staff meeting (the picture on the box shows a woman in a pinstriped suit taking a phone call with suction cups attached to both her breasts). There are nursing pillows that look like rubber floating rings and nursing "fashions" that make it easy to whip out a boob anytime, anywhere.

Some babies take to breast feeding from the womb. The ease of breast feeding seems directly proportional to how hellish your pregnancy and labor was. I have a friend who had a complicated pregnancy and a gruesome, three-day labor, but her baby clamped onto her nipple without further ado. ("It was the only easy thing in this whole ordeal," swore my friend.) But all too often it's not easy at all, forcing you to muster a mountain of willpower to make it happen. Millions of women either can't make it happen or decide that they deserve just a smidge of relief in their new, exhausted, terrified lives, and opt to bottle feed. This is a perfectly acceptable alternative, despite what Lactation Nazis tell you. Your first task of motherhood, then, becomes finding the strength to do what's right for you and your baby—and ignore all who would tell you otherwise.

THE POOP LIST

Many events occur in the first week of parenthood that do not occur ever again in your life. Among them is the Poop List.

After you've brought your baby home, your pediatrician will take a healthy interest in her eating and weight gain. The idea is to fatten baby up so that she doubles her birth weight by the six-week checkup. Conversely, what comes out the other end becomes of great interest as well. The doctor will tell you to keep a strict diary of everything that comes out of your kid until otherwise notified. You and your partner, naturally, are too shell-shocked to argue. You begin a poop list.

Here's how you typically compile the data for such a list:

One of you (but usually Mom, thanks to her new superhuman sense of smell) catches a little whiff of something.

"She's got a poopy!"

The other of you (let's say Dad), rushes to find the pen and paper. "OK. Now how big is it?"

"Um, it's medium big."

"Can you describe it?"

"Kind of like half of an Almond Joy."

"That's pretty big!"

"Well, OK. Half that."

"Is it mustard-colored?"

"Yes. Yes it is. It's mustard-colored with little seeds."

"Texture?"

"A good texture. Creamy, but not too watery."

Strangely, all the literature describes poop in various condiment-related terms. Try not to let this bother you.

After you've recorded all this, maybe even entered it into a spreadsheet database, you'll look at each other and sigh with relief. All the books talk about this mustard-colored poop in the first week, so you're right on target. You're flush with another successful parental duty performed.

You'll be able to do it all again. And soon. Newborns poop and pee an awful lot (they don't have a lot else to do when not sleeping). An average evening's poop list can look like this:

4 A.M.: poop
4:15 A.M.: little pee
4:16 A.M.: little poops
5:20 A.M.: pee
5:30 A.M.: BIG POOP
6 A.M.: (illegible scribble, tear stains)

Your pediatrician will want to hear all about this, so one of you will have to stand at the phone and recite this list, with a straight face.

"OK, last night was good. We had three poops and nine pees. What? Yes, they were decent poops, not that little watery stuff. What? Um, like peanut sauce without the peanuts. Yes. Thank you, we're proud of her, too."

The poop list makes you hard (no pun intended). When you're forced to deal in the minutiae of excrement, it loses its horror fairly quickly. This is good, as you're going to be dealing in poop a lot in the next two and a half to three years. Orange poop. Diarrhea poop. The dreaded two-alarm poop (when both of you need to work together to contain an unusually large amount of the stuff). And on and on.

The good news is that for the first day or two, your little burrito is still pooping meconium, which, although alarmingly black and tarlike in consistency, is pretty easy to clean up. Much easier than spit-up, which tends to cling to clothing and hair (yours). The basic rule to remember about poop is that it generally mimics what went in the other end.

"Try to get one that doesn't spit up. Other than that, you're on your own."

—CALVIN TRILLING

Of course later on, when you've introduced solid foods to your baby, his or her poop will reflect the menu and become ever more adult in texture and smell. Fortunately, Nature waits until you've got more of a grip on parenthood before it springs the serious shit on you. Just wait until your little boy demonstrates a condition known as Explosive Bowel Movement Syndrome, in which he shoots it toward the back wall, splattering you and your pristine nursery in the process.

Stop grimacing. This is what parenthood is all about.

SLEEP DEPRIVATION

Everyone knows newborns don't sleep. We've seen it on sitcoms a million times. We've heard our older siblings talking about how they didn't sleep at all for the first six months of their children's lives. We've watched our new-parent colleagues at work walk into walls (and lie there gratefully for as long as we let them). Sure, it sounds rough, but it doesn't sound that rough. I mean, who among us didn't pull the occasional all-nighter in high school or college?

Fact is, an all-nighter is just that. A single night. If you were in law or medical school, OK, maybe you pulled a back-to-back all-nighter, but you're still no tough guy compared to a new parent. Try one whole week of zero sleep. I dare you. Yeah? Now do a second week. And a third. Scientists have done all sorts of studies on what happens to a person who's not allowed enough REM sleep over a period of time, and the results aren't pretty. They probably do a lot of this research on new parents.

You have but to look closely at any new parents of an under-three-month-old baby to get the picture. Note the glazed eyes. Watch them sway as they stand upright. Marvel at the particularly deep shade of lilac under their eyes, and at the way basic English is beyond them:

"Darling, where's . . . what's her name?"

"Who?"

"You know . . ."

"Your mother?"

"No . . . you know . . . whatzit . . ."

"Your sister?"

"No! You know . . . that little, pink . . ."

"Oh! Little Susie!"

"Yeah! Where is she?"

"Uh, she's sleeping . . . I put her down somewhere . . . isn't she with you . . . ?"

Sleep deprivation merely begins in the first week. Lest you reach the end of your first 168 hours as a new parent with the impression that this isn't so bad, be aware that sleep deprivation is exponential. If you survived the first week with any brain cells intact, by the third week you're sure to be surly and monosyllabic.

One can only wonder what role sleep deprivation played in the evolution of the human species. What sense does it make to destroy the brains of the only two people who care enough to feed this screaming chickenlike thing? But once again Nature proves it's smarter than we are.

Next year, when you're hardened parents with a sturdy one-year-old, break out the evidence of what life was like in the first week—videos, photos, scrawled pleas for help. Look how tiny and frail she was then. Look at the terror in your eyes. Remember how inept and unprepared you felt? You never would have survived the first week if you were fully conscious.

THE "IS THE BABY STILL ALIVE?" GAME

Despite a level of exhaustion that makes your college cram sessions seem Mickey-Mouse in comparison, despite the facts that your reaction time makes you a menace on the roads and your vocabulary is back to fifth-grade levels, all new parents are able to carry out one objective hundreds of times in each twenty-four-hour period: Making Sure Baby Is Still Breathing.

Newborn babies sleep like the dead. And since you are so new at this, you must constantly reassure yourself that this tiny new human is in fact asleep and not dead. You're particularly compelled to do this during the first week, when your terror at having a frail, squalling new member of the human race in the house is still fresh. While it peacefully sleeps, you'll spend much of the day staring into the bassinet convincing yourself that the blankets are, in fact, moving with each exhale. Every now and then, when its breathing becomes so shallow it appears that those blankets are not moving, you'll notice how still and translucent its face is, how cool to the touch its forehead . . . and then it's jostled awake as you dive over the bassinet for the phone to call 911.

This isn't hysterical, hormonal mother behavior. Dads are just as bad—they just try to act nonchalant about it. They'll hide all manner of mirrors and bells underneath the crib mattress for this express purpose, and have no compunctions about waking a sleeping baby just to check in. Let them think you know nothing about this or you'll blow their cover as the calm, rational male of the household.

IDEALS OUT THE WINDOW

Memorize this phrase: Whatever Works. This is your mantra for the first seven days of parenthood. Without it, you will not make it.

Just last week you were a different kind of parent.

You had an exacting plan for parenting your newborn that was culled from nine months of studying the latest child-rearing literature and closely examining what you did and didn't like about your own childhood. You would have the perfect birth, and from there, the perfect mothering experience. There would be no formula for your precious child: he would be exclusively breast fed for the first five years. He wouldn't need a pacifier, nor would you offer one. Father would spend an appropriate amount of time bonding with his child. He would be sleeping through the night by six weeks. From these and a hundred other loving details, you would not deviate.

Ah, and then the baby came. And all that stuff went flying out the window in favor of the all-powerful Whatever Works paradigm. By now, this shouldn't surprise you. After all, didn't the baby come three weeks earlier than planned? And you know what happened to your plans for an all-natural birth. If you're smart, you'll realize that the primary truth on Planet Parenthood is this: children don't give a hoot about your plans. They have their own agenda, which they're prepared to fight for, and that goes for just about everything involved in the eighteen years they're your legal responsibility. They'll fight you on sustenance (Juice. In a bottle. Twenty-four hours a day); choice of toys (you'll cave in about the toy guns); and when and if they're going to your alma mater (No way, you bourgeois pig. I'm joining an ashram.) Didn't you do the same to your parents?

I can see you still think it will be different with you.

Let's look at some of the very first ideals to go, then, shall we?

COTTON DIAPERS

You called around to find the best diaper service with the most ecologically friendly methods for the cheapest price. The week before you're due, the diaper guy comes and delivers you an alarming number of "newborn" diapers. He also gives you a schedule to follow for when to put out the poopy diapers and receive fresh, laundered ones. You set it aside to read it later.

The baby comes home and you discover that the "newborn" diapers are big enough to use as blankets. The same goes for the diaper wraps, which until three days ago you had never even heard of. So you try to fold the diapers over to make them fit better, only to find that now you can't get the safety pins through all that cotton. You're far too scared to try any harder because God forbid you should accidentally stick the baby because it might get infected, she might die . . . You begin to cry. Here it is, the first week, and you can't even diaper your own progeny. You're a failure as a mother. Finally, out of desperation, you concoct something that makes your child look like a queen ant and set her in the bassinet. You try to decipher the diaper schedule, but can't because hormones have ruined your abstract reasoning skills. You suddenly smell a poop (that was quick), unwrap baby, and find her and the diaper covered in mustard-yellow paste. Aim diaper at diaper pail. Miss diaper pail. Clean screaming baby. Try to recreate queen ant diaper arrangement but fail. Husband or mate comes home to find you sitting on the toilet sobbing uncontrollably clutching naked (and peacefully sleeping) baby in arms. He goes to Walmart, buys a bag of the "evil" disposable diapers you were going to shun in handy "newborn" size, brings them home, diapers up the girl, cleans up floor, puts you and girl to bed. When you wake up you're so profoundly grateful you vow to buy stock in Procter & Gamble. Whatever works.

THE FAMILY BED

According to the literature, your baby is supposed to get used to sleeping on his own from day one. But very few parents can manage this. Very soon within the first week, one of you discovers the secret to getting baby to sleep for a few hours each night: letting baby sleep *on* you.

Now, you may have heard about the Family Bed, a philosophy advocating that the entire family—Mom, Dad, baby, siblings, and random pets—sleep together in one big bed. It's only thought of as a "philosophy" by middle-class American parents who could otherwise afford a separate crib for baby but who choose not to. In reality, most of the developing world already sleep in one bed, for warmth if nothing else. But, you weren't about to adopt any such notion in your household anyway, since you fully back the idea of your baby learning to sleep through the night as soon as possible—in his own room.

So one night you're sitting brain-dead in the rocking chair, holding your sleeping child on your chest. Every time you put him down he wakes up and starts screaming again, but as long as there is full body contact, it's la-la-land for all. A plan starts to form in your sleep-deprived brain. What if you get up and lie down in bed with the baby . . . not get under the covers or anything, just lie down on the soft, cool pillows and see if he wakes up. You figure it's worth a try. The baby starts to whimper as you tiptoe back into your room but quiets down immediately as you stretch out on the bed. Now this is the ticket! Why didn't you think of this before? You'll just lie here until he's good and asleep and then you'll carry him back to his own crib. Four whole hours later your wife wakes you with a smile on her face, looking like a new woman. She got five hours of uninterrupted sleep, she tells you, thanks to your brilliant idea of bringing the baby to bed with you. Said baby, meanwhile, is still actually asleep on your chest. Amazing. If you'd have known this six months ago you wouldn't have dropped all that money for a crib. Hey, whatever works.

IN THE MEANTIME . . . WHAT DAD CAN DO

The first week with baby results in two separate sets of experiences—one for Mom, the other for Dad. Mom is a living, breathing hormone, breaking down into sobs every time she glances at her new child. She's in pain. She's exhausted. Her boobs are four times larger than normal, and she's rendered speechless in the face of her overwhelming new responsibility. Dad, on the other hand, isn't getting as much sleep as he's used to.

Don't argue with me here. Everyone knows deep down that it's the woman getting the short end of the stick when it comes to childbirth. In light of this, there are a few things the new dad can do to make himself useful in the face of this gross inequity.

Car seat. Install the damn thing. This isn't easy because car seats, for whatever reason, don't fit into cars, particularly cars that aren't minivans. Some of us think this is a diabolical conspiracy on the part of automobile manufacturers to force us all to upgrade, but there you go. Car seats are notoriously unwieldy, heavy, and complicated to install. When against all odds you angle it into the backseat, you then have to figure out which seatbelt goes into which cranny and which harness goes into which nook. If your backseat has bucket seats, which many, many cars do, nothing you do will make your car seat stable, so you're back to the minivan solution again. Industry statistics show that more than half of consumers who use them fail to install car seats correctly. Obviously, none of this was designed with the average new mom in mind, so it's best if the menfolk do it. They can go punch a wall later.

New dads must keep their mouths shut for at least the first few weeks, unless it's to console us and tell us we don't look fat. Don't bother asking why we're crying; we can't explain it to you. Don't complain about your sore throat or aching butt *because you don't know what real pain is!* Go along with the tacit agreement

♡ ♡ ♡ ♡ ♡ ♡ ♡ ♡ ♡ ♡ ♡ ♡ ♡ ♡ ♡ ♡ ♡ ♡ ♡

THE PHONY WAR

A friend from England related his experience with his first daughter. When they brought her home from the hospital, he tells, it was as if she were still hibernating. She slept most of the time, awakening just long enough to eat, then falling back into a deep slumber. He and his wife, who had read all the books and heard all the tales, had braced for the worst, and so when the first week went by with very little trouble, they relaxed mightily. This baby stuff is not so bad, they thought. Three weeks went by, and suddenly their little baby girl "woke up" and shook the neighborhood with her screams. Her parents, by this time, had let their defenses down, and suffered greatly because of it. He called it "The Phony War," likening it to when the Brits dutifully spent their nights in London's subway tunnels at the beginning of World War II . . . only nothing happened. No sooner did they get lax about spending every night in the subways, however, than the horrible Blitz of London began, resulting in a huge number of casualties.

The lesson here? Maintain battle positions until otherwise notified.

♡ ♡ ♡ ♡ ♡ ♡ ♡ ♡ ♡ ♡ ♡ ♡ ♡ ♡ ♡ ♡ ♡ ♡ ♡

that you will run out to the grocery store, video store, or twenty-four-hour pharmacy at any time of the day or night and for any reason, no matter how irrational. Agree with everything we say. Rub our feet.

Most important for new dads, however, is to overcome your fear and step up to the plate. You may be big and clumsy, but humankind has survived this long with men in the picture. You *can* pick up your newborn without breaking her. Get over your squeamishness about cleaning the poop off your baby daughter's privates and learn how to do the quick change. Do your fair share of walking the floor at night. When you've mastered all of these basics, when you're man enough to get out of bed without being asked after the 3:30 A.M. crying starts, then you've earned the right to kvetch about how hard this all is. And remember, we reserve the right to feel put out and insecure if you do any of this too well.

DING!

Neither of you will likely be aware when seven full days have passed since the birth of your baby. More likely Grandma will call to remind you, ask you how you feel (only possible answer: "Damn tired, thank you"). Congratulations. It's the end of round, er, Week One.

You're starting to get pretty good at swaddling. You know how diapers work, too. Nor are you afraid the baby is going to break into several little pieces in your hands when you pick her up anymore. But the sleep thing is still a problem. Ditto the food thing.

But at least you're on your way. You're breaking in. You've made it through the first week of boot camp, which is what separates the men from the mice (and sometimes the moms from the men). It's full-immersion tactics, and you're up to your neck already. Only fifty-one more weeks to go. You'll be fine, even though it doesn't look like it now.

chapter 2

ADAPTING TO YOUR NEW LIFE-FORM

(Weeks 2–12)

"The contractions may have stopped,
but the labor never ends."

—KELLY, MOTHER OF ONE

So you're starting to get more used to this idea of being a parent. Let me rephrase that. You're starting to breathe normally again since it's been a whole week and the baby's still alive and seems happy enough. You're no longer so afraid to pick her up, and you're pretty sure burping, per se, is harmless. You might be developing the beginnings of a workable night routine that allows for basic, no-frills brain service. You've even perfected a quick, tight swaddling technique that would make a professional tamale wrapper jealous. If things continue to go this well you might audaciously begin to consider emerging from the safety of your own home for baby's first stroll.

Well good for you both. Too bad about the colic.

THE CRYING GAME

Colic? Yes, you know about that, don't you? Those regular bouts of earsplitting screaming that usually

USEFUL TERMS

BABY WEARING A descriptive term meaning the constant wearing of, you guessed it, baby. A movement based on the premise that babies who aren't put down for any reason are calmer and do better on IQ tests.

COLIC Hard to define, but you know it when you hear it.

DIAPER GENIE A brand name for a diaper bin that ingeniously and almost completely masks poopy diaper smells. Note I said <u>almost</u>.

THE FAMILY BED Everyone in the same, comfy bed. Promotes that feeling of family togetherness along with, one supposes, warmth. Only considered a "philosophy" in America, where people routinely have an extra baby room and can choose to use it or not.

start, oh, around the third week or so? Nobody knows what causes it, only that it's afflicted babies since time began. Nobody knows why it affects some babies and not others either. Worst of all, nobody really knows how to cure it. They can give you a new heart, tell you what diseases you're genetically likely to get, and clone your pet sheep, but they can't make a colicky baby stop crying. It's a cruel quirk of science. Obviously the people doing the research aren't parents.

♡ ♡ ♡ ♡ ♡ ♡ ♡ ♡ ♡ ♡ ♡ ♡ ♡ ♡ ♡ ♡ ♡

GAS SMILE Babies don't actually smile in response to something before they're six weeks old, but sometimes you could swear you saw them grinning at you from the bassinet. Nope. Either you were hallucinating from lack of sleep or it was a gas bubble.

SIDS Sudden Infant Death Syndrome; every new parent's nightmare, in which baby goes to sleep just fine and the next time you check in on him he's dead. "Put baby to sleep on his back only" is stamped on the forehead of every new mother these days because of a suspected link between stomach-sleeping and SIDS.

SYRUP OF IPECAC A scary little bottle of vomit inducer you buy and keep around in case baby ever drinks a bottle of lighter fluid, which of course you make sure never happens.

♡ ♡ ♡ ♡ ♡ ♡ ♡ ♡ ♡ ♡ ♡ ♡ ♡ ♡ ♡ ♡ ♡

If you're not sure whether your baby has colic, he doesn't. With colic there's no question. When you've fed baby and changed baby and rocked baby and soothed baby in every way you can dream up and he's still howling and pulling up his little legs like he's got really bad gas—that's colic. You'll know because it kicks in at the same time every evening, right about when other families are finishing dinner and having a

♡ ♡ ♡ ♡ ♡ ♡ ♡ ♡ ♡ ♡ ♡ ♡ ♡ ♡ ♡ ♡ ♡

WHAT YOU'LL NEED (WEEKS 2–12)

☀ SWEATPANTS, SWEATSHIRT. One pair that hide stains well and can also serve as pajamas. You can't be expected to change your own clothes every day during these first twelve weeks, can you? Of course not.

☀ BURP CLOTHS. And plenty of 'em.

☀ A WASHER AND DRYER. Or at least a big sink and a drying rack, for God's sake.

☀ ADVIL. The $30 bottle.

☀ EARPLUGS. In case of colic.

☀ LOTTERY TICKETS.

☀ A STROLLER. Because after your first outing, you'll roam farther and farther afield. This will be your second vehicle, so best make it a sturdy model. With lots of cargo space.

♡ ♡ ♡ ♡ ♡ ♡ ♡ ♡ ♡ ♡ ♡ ♡ ♡ ♡ ♡ ♡ ♡

second glass of wine. You'll know it by the pallor of your spouse's face when he or she hands off the kid for your shift.

What's life with a colicky baby like? "It's the ninth level of Hell," said my friend Mark, not smiling. Take the whole ball of wax, the entire body of reasons behind why life with a new baby is so exhausting in every sense of the word—and triple it. Colic is your very worst fears about parenthood come true. There is little to be joyous about when an inconsolable infant greets you at the door every night and makes you feel even more inept as a parent. "Oh, what have we done?" is the refrain you'll most often moan as you walk the floor at 4 A.M.

Everyone promises your ordeal will be over by the three-month mark, or if not, then certainly by six months. Something about baby's digestive system maturing, or his nervous system . . . whatever. You don't give a hoot as long as he stops screaming. In the meantime, your survival depends on practicing aggressive domestic triage. You must relieve the other parent when his or her shift is up and you must not be late, lest that parent succumb to temptation and leave the baby on a church doorstep somewhere. When your shift is over you should leave the house and sit on a quiet park bench until your sense of hearing returns and you can breathe calmly again. Forget about sleeping for now. Consider investing in some professional-quality earplugs.

"Colic, the Terrible Twos . . . it's all just
preparing you for the teenage years."
— KATHLEEN, MOTHER OF THREE

Repeat this often: that which does not kill you makes you stronger. Tape it onto your refrigerator if need be. And remember that once you've survived colic, if you're still married by then, the teenage years will pale in comparison. When your teenage son comes home with two nipple rings and his tongue pierced, you can laugh and put it into perspective. He's joined a thrash metal band, he says? At least he'll be doing his screaming somewhere else.

As a bonus, medical science promises that babies with colic often turn into children and young adults with driving, focused personalities. Maybe they tell you this to keep you from selling the baby to the carnival passing through, but it may have some truth to it. My friend Mark's firstborn son screamed every single day from 5 to 11 P.M. and then started up again at 3 A.M. He and his wife would take shifts for dinner. Mark would come home from work and relieve Tracy, pale and shaking by then, so she could go into a dark back room and eat a plate of food in relative quiet. A few hours later she'd take over so he could eat dinner. They did this every night for six months. But their now three-year-old is indeed supersmart, articulate, focused, and seemingly well on his way to being a Fortune 500 chief executive. Will he ever pay them back for what he put them through so early in his life? Probably not.

But you can bet revenge will be sweet when he has his first baby in twenty or thirty years, and they can head for the door as soon as the crying starts.

THE FIRST OUTING

The first venture outside is a major milestone in your development as a parent because it involves Herculean feats of strength, courage, and determination, and packing skills.

There's an old wives' tale that says a newborn shouldn't go outside until after six weeks of age. To most new parents in the first week, that sounds like perfectly reasonable advice. Why would you want to take your frail little child outside, where he might catch a germ, or be rained upon, or even be—God forbid—dropped?! Never mind the tiny detail about how much you ache whenever you stand up. At this juncture, you'd be happy to sit on a pillow in your rocking chair where it's safe for all eternity.

But sooner or later, you'll have to do it. Part of becoming a citizen of Planet Parenthood is growing the chutzpah necessary to take the kid out of the house and into his first experiences with the outside world. That's the world out beyond the backyard, I mean.

First, you'll need a compelling reason to leave the house. Let's say you've run out of cranberry juice, which you're either drinking by the gallon because you're breast feeding and continuously thirsty or because it's the only drink you can stomach after labor.

Anyway, you've run completely out, and since your mate is off working and Grandma went home already, it's up to you to run down to the corner market and get some more.

By now you will have forgotten how easy certain preparenthood tasks like this were. You will not be dashing off somewhere at the spur of the moment ever again—at least not for the next ten years or so. You cannot simply slap hand to forehead because you forgot tomato sauce and run right back out to get it. If you forget the tomato sauce now, you'll just have to make do with bread and water for dinner.

But I digress. You need cranberry juice, yes? OK. First things first. You'll need to look at the clock and decide if it's worth packing up the baby and all the gear and getting yourself emotionally ready to step outside before 5:30—when your partner comes home and you can just send him out instead. It's a very real consideration, especially if you've never ventured outside by yourself *avec bébé* before. But say it's noon, and you have a good five or so hours to work with. The second thing you'll have to do is pack baby's bag.

Now, hopefully somebody gave you a good, sturdy diaper bag for a baby present. If not, find your old student backpack or the biggest tote bag in your closet. Hopefully somebody with a little experience gave you a quick seminar in what to put into it. If not, here's a quick primer: diapers, wipes, changing mat, spit-up cloths, change of clothes (or two), extra blanket, extra socks, infant Tylenol, two bottles of milk, small toy, two clean pacifiers (attach a third firmly to baby), camera (just in case you get a gas smile), your keys, your wallet, emergency $20, whatever religious medallions will make you feel safer, and, of course, your pager and cell phone. Make a list because you won't be able to remember any of this tomorrow.

Next, decide what device you're going to use to transport baby. If you live in a city, you can either schlepp an awkward and very heavy baby carrier/car seat contraption or put the baby into one of those crunchy Guatemalan slings and just pray you can find her again in all the folds. I should mention that if you think you're up for a healthy stroll down to the corner market this soon after giving birth, *you're wrong.* How are you going to carry a bag of groceries, your diaper bag, and a seven-pound baby when halfway down the block you feel your stitches popping? Didn't think of that, did you? Of course not; you've never done this before. Take my advice and just drive. Car's big. Safe. It's got lots of storage and a radio that can play soothing classical music. Plus you can sit in it. Store's just on the corner? So what. Drive.

Driving, however, has its own pitfalls. After you've waddled into the garage or the carport or wherever you park your vehicle, you've got to somehow open the door and get your child into the car seat. This in itself is no mean feat considering that your every impulse is screaming at you to hold onto that child with both hands. When you somehow manage to do this, you'll immediately face the next parenting challenge: leveraging yourself into the backseat without the use of your arms (which are wrapped around the baby), and getting baby into the car seat itself. Assuming you managed to get the car seat into the car earlier.

Let's say that you've conquered all of the above. Your newborn is wrapped in three blankets and looks like a little lone meatball in a pot of sauce. The car seat tilts her up at an uncomfortable angle, and the sun is in her face no matter how many of those clever window shades you hang in the back. Naturally, she begins to wail. If you think this will get easier in the months to come, it won't. This is the natural state of a baby in the car.

As you drive to your destination, you will be the textbook example of a defensive driver. Like the joke bumper stickers say, you brake for hallucinations. You snarl at people who don't use their turn signals. You scream obscenities at those who cut you off. When you return home you will write a note to remind yourself to look into Volvo prices when the Sunday papers come.

> "A new child in the house is a great tourist attraction. But unlike Disneyland, the lines are shorter and everyone brings casseroles."
>
> —PAUL REISER

Once you get out of the car there are more dangers. You're still not used to the idea of having a baby on your person, so there's some question about how to get such a fragile little thing from the car to wherever you're headed. That unwieldy car seat carrier again? Or maybe you should just carry her? Whatever you decide, you'll have to then defend her from strong winds, big dogs, bright sunlight, coughing people, smothering strangers, refrigerated aisles, and many other perils of modern life.

In time, you will become stronger, more organized. You'll learn to trust your own grip when getting in and out of the car, and you'll know your grocery bag limit when the kid's strapped to your chest in her Snugli. You'll eventually regain your prepartum driving speed. It won't be long before you could live in the wilderness for a week out of your diaper bag. By this time next year it will only take you half an hour to leave the house on a moment's notice.

THE NEW YOU

Catatonic. Ashen-faced. Dumb with terror. All of these adjectives describe you in the first few weeks after you bring baby home. The good news is that they apply less and less as the weeks move on. As you gain confidence in your ability to keep your offspring alive and thriving, the old you begins to emerge with a new sense of self—you secretly begin to see yourself as a parent. It may be months yet before you feel confident enough to utter such presumptions aloud in public, but to the outside world, your new status is painfully obvious. You might as well be wearing a sign on your back that says, "Vomit on me. I'm a parent."

Sometimes all it takes to jolt your sense of self into its new reality is some light name-calling. My own brother did the job for me. Several days after bringing our new daughter home, I lay on the futon surrounded by my father, dutifully assembling a bouncy chair, my brother, pouring me another eight ounces of cranberry juice, my mother, expertly coddling the new baby, and my husband, sleeping on the floor. My brother looked

♡ ♡ ♡ ♡ ♡ ♡ ♡ ♡ ♡ ♡ ♡ ♡ ♡ ♡ ♡ ♡ ♡ ♡

REGULAR TIME (PACIFIC STANDARD OR OTHERWISE) VS. NEW-PARENT TIME

By now you may have noticed your complete inability to get anywhere on time, no matter how long you give yourself to prepare. You may also have noticed that even though pediatricians deal with new parents every day, they still get touchy when you show up twenty minutes late for a scheduled appointment. Perhaps it's their way of getting revenge for all those late-night calls?

This is the reality of being a new parent. You will never again be on time for anything, and you will simply have to adjust accordingly. The morning staff meeting and the grocery shopping suffer equally, and on weekends you can't even get to the zoo before noon. The reasons behind this phenomenon are utterly unclear. You can work an extra hour into your schedule, have the diaper bag packed, have the baby changed, dressed, and fed and yourself as

♡ ♡ ♡ ♡ ♡ ♡ ♡ ♡ ♡ ♡ ♡ ♡ ♡ ♡ ♡ ♡ ♡ ♡

♡ ♡ ♡ ♡ ♡ ♡ ♡ ♡ ♡ ♡ ♡ ♡ ♡ ♡ ♡ ♡

well, and still not get out the door on time. One possible rationale is that baby has no respect for your schedule and feels he has the right to poop or throw up or swallow a button just as you're about to strap him into the car seat. How to cope? Here are some tips:

☀ Deal only with other new parents. At least they'll buy your excuse. They may even be ten minutes later than you.

☀ Concoct five truly plausible excuses for coming into work half an hour late and rotate them on a weekly schedule. Maybe your boss won't catch on.

☀ Be on continual Code Red Alert. Have the diaper bag packed and ready by the door twenty-four hours a day. Consider buying a few prepackaged, nonperishable energy snacks that can be tossed in and safely forgotten about. When the time comes to leave the house and meet an appointment, you'll have the equipment and the adrenaline necessary to make the attempt. Of course, you will still be late.

☀ Explain to everyone up front that you have a baby with you and so are operating on New-Parent Time. If they grumble, tell them you'll see them in about eight years.

♡ ♡ ♡ ♡ ♡ ♡ ♡ ♡ ♡ ♡ ♡ ♡ ♡ ♡ ♡ ♡

up over the bar counter separating the kitchen from the living room. "Mom," he called.

Mom didn't respond. "Mom," he repeated.

Again she didn't respond, and I started to say something when I suddenly realized that he was looking straight at me.

I was Mom.

I was now somebody's Mom.

Oh My God.

Most people aren't in any hurry to be called parents. For people who aren't already in possession of a child and who don't know better, the title isn't exactly complimentary. The popular image of "parents," thanks to TV and movies, is not exactly one that gives the impression of coolness. Maybe if Joe Camel were to become a dad, men would stop equating the notion of fatherhood with Bermuda shorts . . . but probably not. Hollywood, that bastion of family values, has wreaked most of the damage to our image. Whole leagues of actors and actresses who are neither particularly young nor particularly beautiful vie to play Mom and Dad in detergent commercials or Disney features. Middle-class parents are almost always depicted wearing sensible, beige clothing and vacant, idiotic grins. The men are flustered, balding, and paunchy and the women sport pageboys and wear Hush Puppies flats. Soccer Moms are smiling June Cleavers who happily chauffeur their broods in the family minivan. We all grew up watching Disney's Sunday Night Movie featuring such doddering "parents," and we all vowed that we would die before turning into such creatures ourselves. Even Soccer

Moms are insulted when you refer to them as Soccer Moms.

Alas, all stereotypes have some basis in truth. You're well on your way to beige clothing and sensible shoes. If babies do anything at all, they turn you into an adult faster than you can say Honey, I shrunk the kids.

Babies ground you. They compel you to settle down and start worrying about your future—which is their future, technically speaking. You start thinking about moving out of the hip, edgy part of town into the safer, greener, more suburban part. School districts, term life insurance, and tax credits all become scintillating conversation fodder. For the first time in your life you're really concerned about your employer's benefits package. You need a much bigger apartment, or a house, if you can squeeze it. Backyard space becomes a special consideration, and, deep in your subconscious, so does cargo space. Wait, did somebody say *minivan*?

For a small percentage of folks, these stereotypes alone prevent them from creating progeny. But it's just as well, really, because people who feel the need to obsess about themselves all their lives shouldn't be having children at all. These sorts are usually too pre-occupied with their "inner-children" to give the outside kind any thought.

You, however, have gone and done it, joined in with the tribe of parents—a tragically unhip lot by Holly-wood standards. But by doing so you've joined the real world, which comes with an ungodly amount of hard work and sorrow but also a fabulous benefits package. Your parents signed up for it, after all, and look, now they've got a grandchild to spoil! So did their parents. And their parents. Folks had to do something with their time before TV and the Internet.

Your new role as parents comes with some perks. A residual preindustrial elevation in status comes with bearing children, not unlike that in those tribal societies you read about in *National Geographic*. When a young couple have their first child they are ushered into adult society, the husband can buy a starter-cow, and the wife can look her mother-in-law in the eye without getting beaten. The village elders might even give them a hut of their very own. Here, the elders decide to forgive you your youthful folly (Uncle Al might even forgive you for joyriding his Porsche way back when), and they might be more inclined to help you buy a hut of your own. Bosses at work view you with new respect, now that you're a family man (of course for women it often goes the other way, but we'll get to that). Your car insurance goes down. Your mortgage application looks stronger. Marketers covet your dollars and car salesmen wink as you walk by. It's understood by all who've gone before you that you've finally joined the world of respectable adults. In the public eye, anyway. You're a grown-up. And that scores you points.

GOING NATIVE

If the first week of parenthood was boot camp, the ensuing weeks are the adjustment period. This is when necessity becomes the mother of invention (no pun intended). The reality of having an infant in the house clashes violently with all those ideals you held before you brought her home. Now is the time you're reexamining all your previously held parenting ideals and modifying them for sustainable life on Planet Parenthood. These are the biggies, the practices that will define what kind of parent you become.

Take breast feeding, for example. As in: breast vs. bottle. A Big Issue if there ever was one. Of course you were planning on breast feeding. In America, breast feeding has grown in popularity in the last thirty years, and more recently has become the maternal battle cry of white, educated, middle-to-upper class women choosing to have their children later in life. And for good reasons. Every pediatrician on the planet agrees that "breast is best." It's specially-mixed with your unique offspring in mind, thanks to those all-knowing hormones again. It passes on your immunities to your newborn. It's free. Lactation enthusiasts say it helps you bond with your baby and adds quite a few IQ points to his developing brain as well.

But, as you're no doubt discovering, it ain't that easy. A human baby doesn't know how to suckle in the beginning, so you have to teach it. Maybe yours will catch on quickly and maybe it won't. Maybe you'll decide it hurts too much, and since you're emotionally and physically exhausted or you've already suffered through two breast infections, you may well decide to give the whole glandular thing a miss and bottle feed your baby. It's a perfectly good decision that can make everyone happy. Besides, now you can foist the night feedings onto Dad!

Ah, but you didn't expect all the peer pressure, now did you? These days, some women approach breast feeding with the same gusto they've put into their careers. They will not accept defeat in this arena, and they will not accept it from you, either. If they can deal with the cracked, bleeding nipples and with expressing sixteen ounces of milk during their morning commutes, then so

♡ ♡ ♡ ♡ ♡ ♡ ♡ ♡ ♡ ♡ ♡ ♡ ♡ ♡ ♡ ♡ ♡ ♡

WHO ARE THE PARENT POLICE?

☼ They're the ones who've been staring at you for the last ten minutes.

☼ They're the ones who volunteer that your stroller's been recalled by the manufacturer, and how come you weren't aware of that?

☼ They're the ones who tell you your baby is under-dressed for this weather.

☼ They're the ones who tell you your baby is over-dressed for this weather.

☼ They're the ones shaking their heads when you pull out the baby bottle.

☼ They're the ones who act as if your baby's runny nose is bubonic plague.

☼ They're everywhere, like KGB. So watch out!

♡ ♡ ♡ ♡ ♡ ♡ ♡ ♡ ♡ ♡ ♡ ♡ ♡ ♡ ♡ ♡ ♡ ♡

can you. Unfortunately, a lot of these kinds of women slip over the edge and become Parent Police. They equate bottle feeding with nothing less than child abuse, and they have no qualms about telling you how they feel on the topic. You'll feel their steely glares at the park when you pull out a bottle instead of your breast. They'll ask you if your baby's been sick lately. They'll inquire about your baby's place on the percentile chart, all the while fingering a La Leche handbook with missionary zeal. Worst and hardest of all to take, they question your devotion and ability as a mother.

You hardly need this. Not here, not now. The fact is, there are myriad reasons, all personal and all valid, for why a mother breast feeds or bottle feeds her infant. No mother, already exhausted, already doing her best, needs to be criticized for whatever decision works for her. If the baby is gaining weight and thriving, then the job is being done well, period. Millions of bottle-fed babies grow up not only healthy and smart, but actually manage to bond with their mothers as well.

Of course, having to cough up $80 or more on baby formula *every month* is a very strong argument for giving breast feeding a serious go. A lot of charges, many of them accurate, have been leveled at the giant formula companies in the past. Pharmaceutical companies, which make many leading brands of formula, go out of their way to woo hospitals and new parents with free samples, coupons, gifts, and other enticements. Some hospitals are given huge research grants in exchange for pushing a particular brand of formula to new mothers. It's not uncommon for a new mother to find a congratulatory note and a case of formula on her doorstep just days after leaving the hospital—thanks to a list of live births provided by the hospital to the formula makers. But, not unlike drug dealers, once they have you hooked and hooked good, the freebies stop. And are you going to deny your little baby sustenance? Of course not. You'll hock the furniture if you have to for a fix of formula. One study found that Abbott Laboratories, makers of Similac, raised the price of its product by 207 percent between 1980 and 1993— that's six times the increase in the price of ordinary cow's milk over the same period. The company reaped obscene profits before being busted by federal antitrust investigations. Bottle feeding does have its price, even if it's not the price cited by Lactation Nazis.

Breast vs. bottle is the biggest issue in the minds of new parents—new mothers, anyway. In a lot of ways it's the nastiest, most divisive one. Be prepared to defend whatever decision you make, because both work fine.

Another Big Issue you're finding your way on? Disposable vs. cloth, natch. Before you have a baby you just have no real concept of what it means to change a poop-filled or urine-soaked diaper five or more times a day. This is probably why you thought you'd do the "green" thing and sign up for a diaper service before you ever had your baby, fully intending to diaper your child in tree-friendly, conservation-minded 100-percent cotton diapers. You knew, after all, that disposable diapers fill up 65 percent of the landfills in this great country of ours. Of course, that doesn't factor in the environmental quota exacted by all the chemi-

cal washes commercial diaper services put cotton diapers through to sterilize them, or all the extra energy
you use to wash them and dry them at home. Not to
mention the grim task of trying to pull the poop off
them through repeated dunkings in the toilet. Still, all
the literature assures you that cotton diapers are actually a cheaper alternative to disposable diapers. And
that may indeed be true, providing you opt out of the
diaper service and choose to launder them yourself. For
more details on how much fun that is, ask your Mom
and Grandma.

This battle seems to have already been won by disposable diapers, whatever their evils, since more than
90 percent of American babies now wear them. Very
soon into the birth of a baby, and I mean within a
week, many women quickly come to their senses and
opt for convenience over environmental ideals (this is
America, after all). The few holdouts who insist on
continuing with the cotton diapers soon come around,
however, after realizing that they're changing their
baby four times an hour to your once. Cotton diapers
get wetter, quicker, so that every little pee your baby
has ends up soaking not only the diaper, but his clothes
and your lap. Another result of doing it the environmental way? Preindustrial-style diaper rash. Not fun.
Not pretty.

But for all their convenience, disposable diapers do
cost a pretty penny. And the diaper makers are no
dummies. In the style of formula makers (and tampon
makers and saline solution makers), they know you
can't go without, so you pay a premium. As your baby

♡ ♡ ♡ ♡ ♡ ♡ ♡ ♡ ♡ ♡ ♡ ♡ ♡ ♡ ♡ ♡

BODY LANGUAGE

Babies are a bawdy lot. They do all the same
bodily things adults do, only, being babies, they
don't try to hide them. They poop, pee, fart, play
with themselves, and wipe their noses with their arms,
and you, being their parents, love them all the more
for it.

But because there is so much, um, effluvia, involved with having a baby around, parents must develop a household language for dealing with various
situations. For example: How do you describe a diaper
change? Do you use childish terminology: <u>Susy has a
poopy bum-bum doesn't she?</u> Or do you prefer a more
euphemistic approach: <u>I smell a dirty diaper</u>. And
what do you do about genitalia? There are many col-
orful names to choose from, but which of them are
right for describing your own baby's?

Be prepared. The words you choose for these sorts
of things may one day come back to haunt you. Many
years ago I baby-sat a three-year-old girl whose parents had always insisted on teaching her the correct
words for everything. One day at a neighborhood
gathering the girl came up and very seriously and
loudly asked my boyfriend if he had a penis, like her
brother and her daddy did. I couldn't tell who was
more red, my boyfriend or her father.

♡ ♡ ♡ ♡ ♡ ♡ ♡ ♡ ♡ ♡ ♡ ♡ ♡ ♡ ♡ ♡

grows, the number of diapers in each pack shrinks. A pack of 44 ultrathin disposable diapers for, say, $10, will last you at least a week, but by the time your one-year-old is wearing size 4 or 5 diapers, it's $13 for a pack of 26, which won't last three days. In desperation, you'll start searching the stores for diaper sales or an acceptable cheaper off-brand. Often, the off-brands are off for a reason, but occasionally you'll run into a supermarket brand that works as well as the premium makers', and when you do you will rejoice. You'll call all your new-mom friends and tell them to come over right away so you can clean out the store.

Whatever route you choose, get used to it. You'll be dealing with diapers for the next couple of years at least. Your house will never smell the same again.

Finally, the pacifier question. Do you or don't you? Only the bags under your eyes reveal the truth. Binkies, dummies, suckies, ga-gas—whatever you call them in your household—shut baby up like nothing else can. And as you're quickly learning, when baby is happy, everybody is happy. Trouble is, some people find them indefensible (I suspect most of these people aren't parents). There is a camp out there who feel that these plastic devices are a crutch that should never be introduced to baby lest it lead to nipple confusion and poor nursing. If the baby is getting enough to suck then he'll never need a pacifier, the argument goes. Furthermore, they say, a pacifier will hamper a baby's natural tendency to vocalize and discourage his sense of adventure, as it distracts him from mischief by keeping him preoccupied with what's in his mouth. Critics will usually throw in the "buck tooth" argument for good measure. Nobody likes a glazed-over, "plugged-up" baby.

Except the baby, that is. It's medically proven that infants need to suck. They enjoy it. It comforts them. Sometimes they want to suck even when they're not hungry, in which case, a pacifier will do the trick like nothing else. A lot of new parents start out with negative impressions of constant pacifier use, only to embrace the truth of the matter when they find a pacifier is the only thing that will calm their fretting two-month-old and help get her to sleep at night. The baby might indeed grow attached to her binky and there may well be an "issue" in weaning her from it in future months. But in just as many instances, a baby will lose interest in it altogether before the first year. You just never can tell. It's a control issue, and if you're still trying to maintain control at this point, I suggest you give up now. Resistance is futile. Surrender and join us.

VULNERABILITY RAG

As if you don't have enough to worry about already.

There's nothing like having a child of your own to make you see—in full Technicolor—just how ugly the world really is. As soon as you hold your fragile newborn in your arms, your perception of the outside world takes a giant step to the right. Suddenly what you want more than anything is economic stability, national safety, and a return of societal morals.

The number-one priority of your life has ceased to be your job, your relationship with each other, or the perfect omelette. Your most pressing worry has become keeping this tiny, defenseless human being alive for as long as possible. Or at least until you can get a smile out of him. If you think this constant fretting will go away once the baby reaches his one-year mark you have been grossly misinformed. We've got a million jokes, a million cheap shots at parental worry because it's the root affliction of parenthood. Nobody ever comes out and says it, so let me be the first:

You will be worried sick about this child until the day you die. (Which will hopefully be long before he does, you hasten to add.)

If your baby makes it to one, your deathly fear of SIDS will be replaced with a deathly fear of him falling down the stairs, or toddling out in front of a speeding sports-utility vehicle. When he's five years old you'll be worried about school bus crashes, or lunatics executing their God-given right to bear automatic weapons and shoot up schoolyards. When he's nine you'll worry about abduction, and when he's twelve you'll stay up nights worrying about leukemia. When he's sixteen . . . oh God, don't even go there yet.

And so on and so on. It won't ever go away. Those new furrows in your brow? They won't either.

Women have the leg up on men in this regard, having spent years being offended and saddened by the sorry state of the world. For millions of normal, all-American guys, though, having a child suddenly gives them something to protect and worry about for the first time in their lives. Mention a kidnapping in the news to a bunch of guys, and you might get a few shaking heads and some grumbling about how bad crime is these days, but before long the talk turns back to the game. Mention the same to a group of new dads, however, and notice the animal difference. Eyes narrow. Fists clench. Voices lower. Arguments against capital punishment dissolve into vapor. Everyday risks take on huge new proportions. *What if somebody runs a red light and broadsides me on the way to the grocery store? What if a pack of wild dogs attack us in the park?* Media-invented risks are even worse: Bacteria in the home! Alar on the apples! Killer peanuts!

The media, in fact, are now your worst enemy. You can hardly enjoy the morning paper anymore without stumbling upon some horror story about abused children that ruins your day. Nor can you watch anything on TV or on the big screen that involves children getting hurt, which rules out most of what Hollywood has to offer. You can't get on airplanes anymore. The thought of chemical warfare keeps you up at night. To your new way of thinking, your every ache and pain is surely metastacizing bone cancer. You worry about terrorists targeting your baby's day care. You fret about the cigarettes and beer your newborn won't be abusing for another thirteen years yet.

You can now understand perfectly why your parents reacted the way they did to some of your more dramatic teenage antics. Indeed, you can hardly stand to think of your tiny, innocent little baby doing any of the things you did: the partying! The sneaking out at all hours of the night! That . . . stolen car! You felt so immortal at seventeen, but as you're realizing now, for the first time, that feeling doesn't extend to parents.

By joining the tribe of parents, you gain entrée into a whole new world of pain and concern. Every picture of a kidnapped child's parents sobbing on the front page of a newspaper chokes you up. You stop and make sure unaccompanied children get across the street safely. You even react differently to international events. When Princess Diana died in 1997, the first re-action from every parent I know wasn't "I wonder what she was wearing!" but "What's going to happen to William and Harry?" You couldn't even watch the funeral if you had kids of your own.

It's a tiresome new addition to your life, this con-stant worry, but get used to it. Worry is part and parcel of life on Planet Parenthood, and it's ultimately the sole secret behind why people who have kids look ten years older than people who don't.

CORE INCOMPETENCIES

Like it or not, you will find in the course of this first year that there are certain skill sets your mate has that you don't. That means that while you may be able to soothe a screaming baby, he will only eat peas for Daddy. Or that while Daddy can be trusted to maintain a calm de-meanor on long road trips with baby, you are the one who remembers to pack the baby Tylenol and the pink, not the blue, rubber elephant that he sleeps with.

♡ ♡ ♡ ♡ ♡ ♡ ♡ ♡ ♡ ♡ ♡ ♡ ♡ ♡ ♡ ♡ ♡

THE RECKONING
(How Old Is Baby?)

What's the difference between a twelve-week-old and a three-month-old? Nothing at all. But for some reason, new parents speak in terms of weeks instead of months when they have a newborn. This is probably because twelve is a bigger number than three, and a twelve-week-old baby seems so much healthier, so much bigger . . . so much more likely to stay alive, than a mere three-monther.

If up until now you couldn't tell the difference between a two-month-old baby and a two-year-old, don't despair. It's the kind of calculation only parents can make, and it's guaranteed to become much easier for you as the year goes on. For now, here's a tip: count age by weeks up until three months. After that it gets too confusing, and you have to switch to reckoning in months. Only weirdos refer to children over three years in terms of months, although the more intense type of parent will still use fractions: My son is 3.257 years old. Ignore them. I always do.

- ☼ 6 weeks = a month and a half
- ☼ 12 weeks = three months
- ☼ 24 weeks = six months
- ☼ 12 months = one year
- ☼ 18 months = a year and a half
- ☼ 24 months = two years
- ☼ 36 months = three years

♡ ♡ ♡ ♡ ♡ ♡ ♡ ♡ ♡ ♡ ♡ ♡ ♡ ♡ ♡ ♡ ♡

This is irksome to many women, who naturally feel that since they birthed the baby, they should be the only one who can determine, then satisfy, his every need. Dads have their pride, however, and many a modern man sets out to prove that he can change a diaper or manage a bedtime all by himself. He'll do it well, too—but he'll do it his own way, which is always going to be the wrong way in the eyes of the other parent.

It's worth noting that babies, like little samurai warlords, seem to understand that playing you two off each other results in a better situation for them. Diabolical, yes. But clever, in a Darwinian way.

I'm going to be a sexist dog for a moment and suggest that in the very beginning, it is the woman who appears to be the most naturally skilled at the baby game. But this is usually only because it is more often she who stays home with baby in the early months. Learning all the bells and whistles involved in baby care involves the same fundamentals that apply to golf and driving: practice makes perfect. So what if the first few weeks at home with your new baby are spent sitting in your rocking chair watching the shadows move across the far wall? You're spending all your time with him. Naturally you're going to pick up on some of his inborn idiosyncrasies: which burping method works best, how much he poops, what time of the day he seems most alert, and what his favorite CDs are. Your husband comes home after eight or so hours elsewhere and understandably gets grumpy when you tell him the baby prefers early Beatles to Motown.

I have friends, let's call them Pam and Peter, who almost didn't make it through this early period of one-upmanship. Both are overeducated professional sorts who have no shortage of confidence in their abilities. Their first baby, however, taxed those abilities to the limit. Peter would pick up his daughter clumsily, having not yet perfected the sweeping under-the-head-and-butt method, and Pam would lay into him for being such a clod. Pam, who was staying home with the baby for six months before returning to work, had clued into the various meanings of her daughter's cries, and would let her go on when she deemed it was a regular fussy 6 P.M. cry instead of a more serious variety. Peter would come home from work and watch with horror as his wife seemingly ignored their offspring's desperate cries. He'd make a cutting remark asking what she did all day if she wasn't attending to the baby and pick up his daughter, which in turn infuriated Pam. They had the nastiest, most bitter fights in those first few months, each one convinced the other didn't know what the hell he or she was doing when it came to baby care. In the end, they converged on the same page. Both learned to relax a great deal, and indeed are still married today, even though their now thirteen-month-old daughter will only allow Daddy to read the ceremonial bedtime story.

As your baby grows and gets more complex, you'll have to wrap your head around the concept that he or she will have a different relationship with each of you. By around six months, or whenever he starts to grasp the meaning of "stranger" vs. family, he's got the number on both of you. He expects Daddy to play with him differently than Mommy. He goes to Mommy for the big comfort, to Daddy for the big fun. Or maybe vice versa in your house. Sometimes he'll demonstrate a distinct preference for one or the other, and you'll have to pretend to be an adult about it and not go pout in the corner. Either way, if you love your kid, your kid loves you, no matter whom he's throwing his chew toys at.

Hi Mommy, Hi Daddy

Remember those old black and white movies about Ma and Pa Kettle? Remember scratching your head and wondering why Grandpa and Grandma referred to each other as "Mother" and "Father" even though their children had long ago matured and moved out? There seemed to be no clear reason for it, except for possibly being some secret code meant to throw you off the trail of what they were really talking about. If you remember any of this, then you might be genuinely horrified the first time you yourself call your mate by that moniker. A slip, you'll think to yourself. A cute little in-joke between yourselves that won't happen again. But it will happen again, and it will happen often, and pretty soon, by the end of the first year, you'll almost never refer to each other in the presence of your child by your given names. Wave bye-bye to Linda and Bob. Say hi to Mommy and Daddy, who will one day morph into Mom and Dad, or The Folks or Ma and the Ol' Man or even The 'Rents, but who will never again be known in family circles as Linda and Bob.

This strange new usage sneaks up on you. You'll hardly use it at all in the first few weeks, when baby isn't doing much more than eating, sleeping, and crying, and when you both still see each other as a means to get through this ordeal alive. It will be a rare, loving, and utterly understood-as-a-joke moment when you look to the other and say, "That's a beautiful baby, Daddy," and he says, "Thanks, Mommy." Aw, how touching.

It's not long, however, before this baby begins to take on some characteristics of an actual human being and starts looking you in the eye, expecting things from you, his parents, and you start this name-calling thing in earnest. It falls into place without either of you noticing until it's far too late, but it does so because it has a clear use in your new lives. It quickly and efficiently communicates a wide range of demands and expectations, most of which had no bearing on your old, childless lives but have everything to do with your new situation.

For example, just last year, before you were parents, the sentence "Daddy, will you come in here and help me with this bath?" meant that somebody was about to get real lucky. No longer. Now such a statement, especially uttered in the first year of parenthood, almost always means this: "I'm calling on YOU, THE FATHER OF THIS CHILD, to come hold her down while I shampoo her hair, damnit."

Referring to your mate as Mommy or Daddy packs a

wallop in pure linguistic terms. By putting
moniker in front of almost any phrase, you're
to the family unit, with all the responsibilitie
guilt incumbent therein. On a lazy Saturday afternoo
you may choose not to jump at the request "Sue, could
you come here for a minute?" called from the down-
stairs den. But "Mommy, could you come here for a
minute?" infers that not only does your husband need
you, but your child does as well. And you'll jump, because, after all, you're now a mommy.

Such monikers also help shore up your new views of
each other. To guys, pregnancy, childbirth, and beyond
are largely a big, scary mystery. At least we women
have millions of years of biological precedent helping
us along. But it's all a big blank to men, so it helps
when they can put a name they understand to it. Most
new fathers are hugely impressed, even in awe of, their
wives' new status as "mother." They remember all the
secret powers their own moms possessed, and Lo! here
they are, incarnate in their own women!

The labels also serve to reinforce your identity in
baby's eyes. People who read way too many self-help
books may want their small children to call them by
their given names, but the rest of us can't wait for that
first "Ma-ma" or "Da-da" and the electric thrill it will
bring. And how else is the little nipper going to learn
who you really are unless he hears it from you day in
and day out? Just keep in mind that "Da-da" is easier to
say than "Ma-ma," and as such, Dad will probably be
the first parent your child chooses to address. Plan your
emotional breakdowns accordingly.

ommy and Daddy works just ... private. *It's when it gets out in* ...barrassing. There will come a *...ll slip up and refer to your mate* ... front of a group of friends. If ... aspire to join you on Planet ...ay, you may escape with rings of "Awwwww! That's sooo cute!" Your single friends, however, will fall out of their chairs in hysteria. You can bet they'll have spread your gaffe far and wide by the next day, too. Don't be surprised if your burly coworkers greet you the next morning with "Morning, Daddy" and smart-ass grins on their lips. Nobody ever makes fun of a Mommy, however. It's just another one of those parental double standards.

MARKETING AND YOU

When I was first pregnant, I subscribed to a parenting magazine, reasoning that I should start learning something about this baby business before I actually had one in the house. I never suspected for an instant that by doing so I was offering myself up as a virgin sacrifice to the all-seeing, all-knowing marketing database in the sky, and that in a matter of days giant corporations like Disney and Johnson & Johnson would have not only my name, but my home phone number, my due-date, and the top five girls' names off my A-list. Unless you're prepared to go off the grid, in this day and age it's almost impossible to escape the notice of consumer goods companies once you become a parent. By dint of your fertility you have become an uber-consumer, and they want to tap into those dollars and will, whether you want them to or not.

Part of what makes this so diabolical is the fact that it starts out so innocently. They don't seek you out, you go to them, often because newly pregnant women can't pass up an opportunity to tell everyone about their condition, or because you genuinely want to become a better, more informed parent. So at your first prenatal examination you happily sign up for the "Welcome Club" newsletter (sponsored by the formula companies), or send away for the free baby magazine (sponsored by the pharmaceutical companies), or join a baby shower registry at a department or discount store (which in turn sells that list to other marketing companies). Even your diaper service gets into the game. And once your name gets out there, it's a free-for-all. These companies are banking on their hunch that you, as a soon-to-be or brand-new parent, are willing to spend whatever it takes to make your little one happy/stimulated/well fed. In general, their hunch is right.

There's nothing like having a baby to change a couple's spending priorities. According to the Bureau of Labor Statistics Consumer Expenditure Index, the arrival of the first child is a major "lifechange" that marketers salivate over like nothing else. Spending patterns veer away from new cars and entertainment toward more prosaic items such as housing, clothing, and food. Although new families don't spend the bucks they used to on entertainment (would you rather nap or see a movie?), information—in the form of books, videotapes, and seminars—is a category that spikes rather dramatically upward around this time. Ditto spending on child-rearing products: furniture, toys, accessories. Married couple families account for 70 percent of total consumer spending. The biggest spenders—couples with children under 18—account for 30 percent, and that share is growing.

Once upon a time, new parents bought a crib, a stroller, some onesies, and that was that. No longer. These days, new parents spend nearly $400 billion annually on infant and baby products. Although the birthrate is declining slightly, older parents are making up for it by spending three times as much on their babies as their parents did on them.

That's why you now find yourself trying to juggle your infant with the mountain of junk mail you find in the mailbox every day. They're trying to sell you books and formula and wooden toys from Sweden. They want you to subscribe to the new baby magazine or to try the latest high-tech diaper. Credit card companies write to remind you of your new responsibilities as a parent and offer you a new line of credit with a low APR. Mutual funds and stockbrokers call you during the day to find out how you're going to pay for college.

Just get used to this. They've got you pegged, and they have your baby's birthdate, so you can expect to receive unsolicited parenting crap in the mail from now until you retire. After months of silence, I recently got a shrink-wrapped diaper sent to my house—a new kind that supposedly prevents diaper rash—and it was addressed to my two-year-old daughter. Sigh. I was disgusted, sure. But I kept it anyway, because I'm a parent and I know you can never have too many emergency diapers hidden around the house.

No matter how thrifty you are when it comes to the big-ticket items, the reality is that you will spend mucho dinero on countless little things that you just can't resist buying for your little one. Stuffed animals. Books. Bath toys. Musical jewelry boxes and Lionel train sets and bedroom posters and crib comforters and soccer balls and all manner of silly things our babies don't need but which we purchase because we love our children so much. It's how good Americans in a consumer society demonstrate love. We've been conditioned for this since our own births, and now we're powerless to stop it. So when you do fall prey to the great marketing juggernaut, don't feel guilty. Blame society.

How do you feel so far? Tired, you say? Overworked? Underappreciated? Heck, you ain't seen nothin' yet.

chapter 3

ADVENTURES IN MATRIMONY

(3–6 Months)

"Nothing kills an erection faster than a baby's cry."

—ANONYMOUS

Having a baby changes your relationship with each other more than any other single event. The common wisdom holds that as a couple, you'd better have your relationship in order before you have a baby, because any aspect of it that's not bolted down is going to be blown away in the coming chaos. But, like cutting down on sugar and paying off your Visa card, that's advice most folks heartily agree with but don't put into practice. How many single parents have you heard lamenting, "We were growing apart so we thought a baby might bring us back together . . ."?

Nope. I hope I'm not the first to tell you that the one thing having a baby will not do for your life is make it easier. That goes for everything from paying your bills to keeping up with the laundry, but especially for your relationship as a couple. Mere minutes after the birth of your first baby, neither one of you much resembles the person the other married. You don't re-

♡ ♡ ♡ ♡ ♡ ♡ ♡ ♡ ♡ ♡ ♡ ♡ ♡ ♡ ♡ ♡ ♡

USEFUL TERMS

CROUP A loud, seal-like bark that comes from your child and scares the pants off you late at night. Don't worry, though. It sounds much worse than it is.

SNUGLI An expensive Swiss-made baby harness that lets you hang baby on your front as you go about your day.

TEETHERS Anything ok for your baby to put in his mouth is a teether. This includes plastic teething toys, ice cubes wrapped in washcloths, uncooked carrots, and, of course, your car keys.

UMBRELLAS AND JOGGERS Types of strollers. You can collapse an umbrella stroller to take on a bus, for example. But if you prefer to run to where you're going, buy a baby jogger.

♡ ♡ ♡ ♡ ♡ ♡ ♡ ♡ ♡ ♡ ♡ ♡ ♡ ♡ ♡ ♡ ♡

member marrying your mother or father, do you? But this is essentially what you've done, and all because you decided to up and have a baby. You may ask: how can something so small be such a huge force? Wiser people than you have been pondering that one for years. Best to adapt any way you can. Just remember, you're in this together, figuratively and biologically speaking. So dust off your sense of humor and perspective and love for each other and don't take them off again for the next eighteen years. And don't say I didn't warn you.

THE WAR OF ATTRITION

Whoever coined the phrase "the daily grind" surely had children. For domestic life with a baby does indeed take on a monotonous, grinding regularity that childless households can't imagine. The number of demands placed on your time has tripled. No longer are the hours between work and sleep your own. The baby owns them, and the baby doesn't care if Monday Night Football overlaps with his bathtime. There are clothes to be changed and dinner to be made (no more grabbing a bagel for dinner after work—you've got a baby to feed). There are baths to be given and stories to be read and hours worth of crying to deal with. By the time baby is down for the night, your energy and motivation to tidy up, do a little office work, pay bills, or write letters are down as well. Most likely you'll spend another hour staring at the TV or flipping through a magazine until you both fall asleep on the couch at ten o'clock. This will be your standard weeknight at home for years to come.

Your weekends are toast, too. A few foolish souls try to keep up their former levels of activity. But they very quickly realize the folly of their ways. Go ahead and take your infant to Tahoe, or camping, or on a drive up the coast. And let me know how much fun you all had. The mind-numbing routine of sleeping, feeding, pooping, changing, feeding, pooping, changing, napping,

♡ ♡ ♡ ♡ ♡ ♡ ♡ ♡ ♡ ♡ ♡ ♡ ♡ ♡ ♡

ACCESSORIZE, ACCESSORIZE, ACCESSORIZE

When you have your first child, your refrigerator ceases to be an appliance you keep food in and turns into a bragging board. Layers of photos, starting with the very first, usually very ghastly postbirth photo they took at the hospital, encrust the front. (Please keep any during-birth snaps in a box somewhere out of the kitchen.) Why the refrigerator? Plastic ABC magnets tend to melt on the dishwasher and the microwave is too high. Bedecking the family appliances is only the beginning of your new and unfathomable urge to accessorize. You'll want all manner of tchotchkes that just a few years ago you regarded as tacky, low-rent, or worse. Here's a short list of accessories you'll be coveting as a new parent:

♡ ♡ ♡ ♡ ♡ ♡ ♡ ♡ ♡ ♡ ♡ ♡ ♡ ♡ ♡

feeding, pooping, changing, playing, napping, ad nauseam, continues no matter where you are, and you'll soon learn that it's easier to stay at home and take turns.

But even taking turns takes its toll. In the midst of your new, blindingly monotonous day-to-day existence, something has to give. Both of you will become mercenary and do whatever it takes to snatch yourselves a little downtime. If you're not yet a parent you might gasp at this sentiment, because you plan on giv-

☀ Baby portrait key chain. It doesn't matter if the portrait was taken by Ansel Adams or Kmart, you want it on a key chain.

☀ Coffee mug with baby's picture on it under the legend "I wuv Mommy" or "Daddy's little girl." Your coworkers won't dare snigger about this. Not to your face.

☀ Family portrait mouse pad.

☀ Brag book. So you can show your little darling to anyone who doesn't ask.

☀ Baby photo greeting cards. By using these for the first time this year, you're setting a precedent. All the relatives will expect them from now until baby becomes a surly adolescent and refuses to sit for them anymore.

☀ A "Baby on Board" sticker for your car. Yes, they still make these.

ing nothing short of 110 percent of your time and devotion to your child. Of course you are. Talk to me in six months.

Haven't you ever wondered why so many parents of two-year-olds appear deaf to their child's constant whining? They're not being bad parents, they're just *coping*. Seasoned parents know when to jump and when to ignore as a matter of personal survival. They can tell the difference between the I'm Bored cry and the I Just Shut the Door on My Hand cry, and respond appropriately. You will, too, eventually. You know it's starting to happen when you stop jumping at every grunt your new baby utters, and when you finally learn that leaving a damp diaper on ten minutes too long isn't the same thing as child neglect. When both you and your mate reach this point together, a whole new family dynamic is put into motion. I call it the War of Attrition.

Let me give you a textbook example of the War of Attrition, as practiced at our household. We're sitting in the living room after dinner playing with Annie. I catch a whiff of something foul. "I smell a poop," I say, ostensibly to no one in particular but really aimed at my husband, who pretends he doesn't hear. I don't make a move to change her. Instead, I throw mental brain waves at him, listing the number of child-care tasks I've completed in the last twenty-four-hour cycle that render me morally exempt from the one on hand now. I did the grocery shopping today, after all. And the laundry last weekend. Plus I dealt with the baby

♡ ♡ ♡ ♡ ♡ ♡ ♡ ♡ ♡ ♡ ♡ ♡ ♡ ♡ ♡ ♡ ♡ ♡

THINGS YOU CARE ABOUT

Once upon a time, you got excited about the normal things: Nordstrom shoe sales, big promotions, two-week Hawaiian vacation packages for $999. But now you're a parent, and your excitement bar has dropped. It's the little things in life that thrill you now. Here's a sampling of what can make you do the Happy Happy Joy Joy dance in your inaugural year as a parent:

☀ When your newborn regains her birth weight and then some by the two-week checkup
☀ Five whole hours of uninterrupted sleep
☀ A practically new Peg Perago stroller at a garage sale for $5
☀ Spacious vehicles
☀ Fading stretchmarks
☀ Clean, well-maintained parks
☀ Tupperware in neat little nesting sizes
☀ Baby Gap sales
☀ Finding out that you already live in a good public school district
☀ Grocery shopping—by yourself
☀ Free day at the zoo
☀ Two-for-one Jumbo-Pac diaper sale at Target

♡ ♡ ♡ ♡ ♡ ♡ ♡ ♡ ♡ ♡ ♡ ♡ ♡ ♡ ♡ ♡ ♡ ♡

solo for five hours on Sunday when he had to go into work for a few hours—where it was peaceful and he could enjoy multiple cups of coffee and stimulating adult conversation. I also get bonus points for cleaning up the molding smashed banana we found under the couch this morning.

He doesn't budge, however, because he has a list of his own, no matter how tenuous it might appear to me. Didn't he give her a bath just last night? And doesn't he read her *Going on a Bear Hunt* fifteen times each night? Didn't he endure numerous viewings of the Teletubbies on Saturday morning when I went to yoga? Who empties the Diaper Genie, anyway? And who cooked dinner every night for the last week, hmm?

And so we sit, basking in the aroma of this evening's steamed carrot surprise, each commenting after another five minutes that "somebody's got a poopy" but neither of us doing anything about it. Ultimately, however, one of us will blink, succumbing finally to that primary parental motivator: guilt. What kind of parents leave their daughter standing in poopy diapers for half an hour? Not us, I guess. Luke puts down his tea and starts to lure the girl into the bedroom for changing. The War of Attrition is over for now. But tomorrow is bath night again.

IN SICKNESS AND IN HEALTH . . . BUT MOSTLY SICKNESS

The War of Attrition applies to all aspects of raising baby except for one notable exception—when baby is sick.

Sick?! I hear you quiver. My darling is never going to get sick! Oh contraire, *ma mère* et *mon père*. There will come a time—most likely between the hours of 2 and 5 A.M.—that your baby will wake up sick. Very sick.

There will be a cry that's not quite right coming from the crib. You'll be able to tell because that's one of your strange new-parent powers. Both of you will get up and stand over his crib and wring your hands in worry. One of you will pick him up while the other consults Dr. Spock. Depending on your emotional constitution, it may be as long as fifteen minutes before one of you breaks and runs for the phone to call the Pediatric Hot Line.

This, Grasshopper, is another parental milestone—exposing you to a stone cold fear unlike any you've known before and that you hope to avoid as much as possible in the future. The first time your baby gets one of the many mysterious ailments babies get, your priorities will define themselves as sharply as the Red Sea parting for Charlton Heston. You may have a breakfast meeting with your CEO in a few hours that requires your sharpest thinking and shiniest shoes, but that's on the dimmest back burner at the moment. The vomit can be dripping down your back and the screams waking the neighbors, but all you can think about is *Please, God, let it just be a gas bubble and not spinal meningitis!*

For most parents, the sheer terror of what might be wrong eclipses any thought of inconvenience. Since parents are by definition the most paranoid species on the planet, it's not uncommon for the common cold to take on the appearance of whatever child-crippling illness scares you the most. This goes for strange rashes and scratches as well. I once found a scaly dark scab on my daughter's scalp—*a tumor! Kaposi's sarcoma!!* It was snot mixed with hair.

Telling new parents to calm down and try to have a little perspective is like telling Bill Gates to stop taking over the universe. It's not going to happen. It goes against nature. Every new parent spends much more energy worrying about what could possibly happen than on coping with those sicknesses that actually do. When they do happen, you might surprise yourself with how well you cope, with how handily you remembered the pediatric ward's number off the top of your head.

But you're more likely to panic. Or if not exactly panic, then at least overreact.

My friends Linda and Ben were taking their first trip out of town with their baby daughter, Abigail, in tow when Abby fell and hit her head against the wall trim of the hotel room. "This huge, bluish, blood-filled bump rose on her head," says Linda. "I thought it looked like a hematoma."

A hematoma?! Ben didn't like the sound of that. Although Linda tried to tell him it was just a $5 word for "bump," Ben wanted it looked at by a medical professional. And soon. But HMOs being what they are, they couldn't find anyone who was able to see them before morning. So Ben did what he thought was the responsible next best thing. He called the paramedics. "I figured they could send a guy over," he later told me. "You know, just to make sure she was OK."

Minutes later they heard the sirens. Linda watched in horror as what seemed like the town's entire emergency-response team screamed into the parking lot. Paramedics, firefighters, ambulances, and several police cars. People in nearby rooms poked their heads out of their doors to watch the ruckus. Half a dozen emergency personnel pounded down the hall to their room, where Linda, Ben, and a perfectly petrified Abby sat huddled.

A female paramedic took a close look at Abby's head. "Awww, it's just a little goose egg!" Translation: a hematoma. A bump. Everybody laughed (except for Linda and Ben, who were too mortified), and they all packed up and left—after asking Ben where they could send the bill. The lesson here? Give a phony address.

LITTLE COUGHS, LITTLE FEVERS . . .

Illness is one of the few nasty occurrences you can bank on happening to your child (besides teething and having at least one poop accident on the bedroom rug), and there's not a whole lot you can do about it apart from washing your hands fifteen times a day and amassing a small pediatric medical library.

Babies are little conduits for all manner of viruses and bacterial infections. If they so much as pass another baby on the street they'll bring home every infection that kid has to offer. Parks are also breeding grounds for all sorts of nastiness. And don't even mention day care centers: the Centers for Disease Control in Atlanta should monitor every one of them.

But don't think you're safe if you keep baby away from other babies. Some parents go off the deep end in this regard, refusing to take their babies outside during cold or flu season and not even allowing anyone but immediate family to pick them up. This is a laughable exercise in futility. You'll bring home a little something from the office, and the baby will get sick from you. Social isolation will only hurt the kid and drive you insane, as well as invite comparisons to Howard Hughes. And look at the way *he* ended up.

You'll have to live with baby's illness in more ways than one. More often than not, whatever baby gets he graciously passes on to you. And since he's such an effective little germ-gatherer, you and your mate can plan on getting sick yourselves a great deal more than normal. Sometimes, in a sick twist of fate, the two of you will be bedridden with some awful stomach flu that passes right through baby. The sickest part is, your child-care duties do not get curtailed. There is no sick-day policy on Planet Parenthood. You have to make breakfast and change diapers even if you're semiconscious while you're doing it. And it gets worse as baby gets older and goes out more often and brings home more pestilence and disease for the whole family to enjoy.

You've just got to steel yourself for the fact that babies get sick a lot. But at least you're living in an era of vaccinations and antibiotics that prevent or cure a lot of the biggies. Obviously you don't want to think about this, but one hundred years ago new parents such as yourselves could expect—that's right *expect*—to lose at least one baby to a childhood illness. So put your baby's fever into perspective and go see the doctor.

EXPLAINING YOURSELF TO YOUR SINGLE FRIENDS

The first time you ask your childless friends to wash their hands before they pick up baby, they'll happily oblige. For all they know, that's just standard operating procedure. The second time around, however, they'll raise their eyebrows. And when you ask them not to come over because it sounds like they have a little cold developing . . . well, you're pushing it.

Let's face it: you're just not the barrel of laughs you were before you brought this baby home. Your old friends are really trying to accommodate the new you, but there's only so much they can take. Not only can't you come out and play anymore, but on the rare occasions you can, you can't stay awake past your bedtime and you have embarrassing stains on your clothing.

Somebody has to take the plunge first, right? If you're the first in your circle to have children, then you deserve a Congressional Medal for boldly going where nobody you know has gone before. Alienating your friends probably wasn't something you worried over—or even thought about—back when you decided to get pregnant, but that's the end result. It's one of the first manifestations of new parenthood.

Impromptu shopping sprees with your girlfriends are a thing of the past. Snapping up those Yankee tickets a friend sprang on you? Don't think so, pal. Not unless you're one of the 2 percent of parents in the universe who have a reliable, affordable baby-sitter who's on call 24–7. In fact, the words "impromptu" and "improvisation" are largely wiped from your vocabulary unless you're talking about what to do when you've run out of diapers at midnight on Christmas Eve. You might refuse to accept this at first and continue to act like you're still the same old person, accepting all invites to parties, like I did (*Just bring the baby; she can sleep on the bed with the coats!*). But you soon realize this works better in theory than in practice. You are not the carefree young adult you once were. Now you have real responsibilities that make your old complaints about a demanding job and no free time seem feeble in comparison. Still, in the first month of parenthood you're apt to be shell-shocked. Expect your friends to clue into this new reality of yours before you do. They, after all, are working on a full eight hours of sleep.

You're still loved, of course. Your old friends are still your friends. But after the dust has settled and they've all made the required pilgrimage to see your new baby and finished with their clucking and mewing, they will look to you as if to say, "OK. Now what?" If you can muster complete sentences at all, you have a lot of explaining to do.

Friends after baby (FAB) fall into one of three categories. The first is those who will view you as a grand experiment because they aspire to become parents themselves one day (but not just yet, they hasten to add). These are the people who will come over more than the others. They will bring yet more receiving blankets and probe for more detail about just how bad your labor was. They may even venture to hold the baby.

Many will offer to baby-sit. Some will beg for the honor.

"Go out anytime," she (and it's always a she) will insist. "I'll be right over to watch Junior." Just about everyone who falls into the "I-want-to-have-a-baby-someday" camp will extend this particular offer. And in lieu of another receiving blanket, it's a generous promise.

But you probably won't be taking this friend up on her offer. It's the rare new parent who has the stomach to leave his or her infant in unskilled hands, and at a time when you're still balking at leaving the kid with Grandma, who successfully raised four of you to adulthood, it's best to do yourself a favor and decline. Who needs to grow an ulcer this year, anyway?

It's when you really stop to consider an offer of baby-sitting from a single friend that you realize just how you've changed. Your thinking on the possibility should remain between you and your mate, since although it will alarm you, it will insult your friend.

Let's say Susan, your dear old friend from college, insists on baby-sitting while you take a few hours to go have dinner. Up until now, Susan appeared to both of you to be the very model of a modern woman: smart, professional, competent.

"Susan," your mate might say. "Hmm. Do you think she could handle it? I mean, don't you think she's a little high-strung sometimes?"

"Yes, she is a bit emotional sometimes," you agree. "She might not perform well under emergency conditions."

"And I think she watches way too much TV."

"Not to mention the kinds of men she dates. She might invite one over when we're gone, and then what?"

"You know, I don't even think she can drive a stick shift. What if she needed to get the baby to a hospital?"

"Yeah, and doesn't she dye her hair? I don't want any residual chemicals coming off on the baby."

You politely decline Susan's offer to baby-sit for now but invite her over next time you have a dinner party (in about four years).

The biggest positive to this group of friends? Presuming you're all around the same age, your wanna-be parent friends will observe you closely for a few weeks before embarking on a mad attempt to join you on

Planet Parenthood. When my daughter was three or four months old, I was invited to a dinner with a group of friends and decided to take her (she slept a lot, and we took her out all over San Francisco . . . for the first year, anyway). I have a picture of her being passed around the table so all my married or engaged thirty-something friends could look longingly upon her. Within a year nearly every woman at that table was preggers herself. The strange twist to this story is that now the only one I still talk to is the one woman who's still a non-mom. Go figure.

"What age is best for a woman to have children? Physically, in her twenties; emotionally, in her thirties; financially, in her forties."

—MONICA, MOM OF TWO

The second group of friends includes those who, unlike yourself, have no desire to settle down or get married, and are very much opposed to what you've just done. To them, your little bundle of joy is like a very expensive and high-maintenance car—something you're now obsessed about and fearful of scratching. Something they hope you'll get over soon so you're back to your old crazy self. These might be college or high school buddies with whom you once passed out in gutters, or the girlfriends you danced on tables with every Friday night. Maybe they're members of your band, or your young executive women's group. Whoever they are, the idea of having a child is about as foreign and repugnant to them as signing up for medical experiments. They might pull you aside to earnestly ask you what you were thinking when you brought all this down on yourself.

These kinds of friends will obligingly show up for a viewing, bringing with them a BB gun or some other age-inappropriate toy, glance uncomfortably at the baby, ask to use the bathroom, and then quickly leave, saying they'll call you sometime. And they will call. But more often than not they'll call you every six months or so with an impossible offer, like last-minute outdoor concert tickets, as if just testing the waters to see if you're still tied down to that . . . thing . . . you had last they saw you. Generally speaking, you are.

Sadly, these friends largely fail to adapt to your new circumstances. As time goes on they call less and less. When they do call you have less and less to talk about. You can practically hear them sigh as they dutifully ask how the baby is doing, so you dutifully keep it down to one adjective when in fact you long to gush at length about how he's smiling at you now and looks *soooo* cute in this little bunting you found on sale at Baby Gap. Then there's an awkward silence. Then your friend will find some lame excuse to ring off, and you won't hear from him again for another six months, when he calls to ask if you two want to join him in a day trip to the wine country (the answer will still be No). By the end of the year, this group of friends is all but extinct. Indeed, if any members remain at all they're acting suspiciously like members of the previous group, and there may yet be hope.

The third group is more like a subgenus of friends. These are career buddies, people you met in college or on the job who have always admired you for your edge, your ambitions, or your Rolodex. You were close mostly because knowing each other was mutually beneficial in the jungle of corporate America. Now that you've stepped off the track, they're not sure what to do with you, or where you fit into their career plans. You've only got a few months to redeem yourselves in their eyes. And if it comes to pass that, surprise surprise, your new baby becomes more important than your work, you're already unredeemable. Oh well.

If you have a sense of humor, these friends can provide a rich source of entertainment for as long as they still come around. One such friend came to visit me one day several months after the birth of my daughter. She surveyed my sloppy apartment, eyeballed my stained leggings and soggy T-shirt (I hope she didn't notice the mismatched socks), and asked me, in all seriousness, "So, what is it you do with your time now that you're not working?" Another assumed I now had the time to take tennis lessons.

These people have no clue. And since you can't begin to explain to them (or indeed to yourself) what it is that keeps you from taking a shower until 4:30 each afternoon, don't even try. Save your brain cells for other, more important things, like remembering to eat. They'll learn the truth of things when and if they ever have kids.

THE CARE AND FEEDING OF NEW-PARENT FRIENDS

Clearly, you need a new set of friends.

Since your social life will, from now on, be severely compromised, the only solution is to adapt to a new version. This means finding—and keeping—new-parent friends. This is crucial to your future well-being. As we've established, while your old friends are still fond of you, they understandably don't want to hang out much anymore. They don't want to hear about your son's amazing projectile poops. Your scheduling problems only irritate them. And they know you're not listening anyway. By the time your baby can pull the phone socket out of the jack in the middle of a friend's traumatized retelling of the date from hell, she's either used to it or won't bother calling anymore.

You need friends who are on the same page (or is it diaper?) with you in every way. You need friends who can, with a minimum of sleep, opine about nipple confusion and distinguish between stroller brands. In short, you need new-parent friends.

Nobody knows how you feel right now more than those who also have a new baby. They are also sleep-deprived. They are also in a state of almost constant alarm, overly concerned with how warm the room should be, how long to nurse at each breast, how to assemble a baby swing, etc. New-parent friends complete the troika of experts all new parents need to get through this year (grandparents + Dr. Spock + new-parent friends).

But finding new-parent friends is easier said than done. Firstly, having a baby does not by itself mean you have enough in common with another couple to forge a friendship, so the trick is to find people you'd like even without a baby on their arm. Trouble is, people hit all sorts of unsavory extremes during their first year as a parent. People tend to revert to type, no matter how many years of therapy they've completed. Type A personalities get more so, trying to keep a schedule and feed baby, down to the ounce, exactly by the book. They don't see why they can't continue to breast feed exclusively while holding down a full-time job as a corporate lawyer, and they'll just about kill themselves trying. Parenthood isn't going to break them or hamper their dynamic lifestyle, by gum. (Nervous ticks or a live-in nanny are a sure sign that it has.) Meanwhile, the more laid-back Type Bs don't even try to save themselves as they're sucked into the chaotic vortex of parenthood. They lose all sense of self, fashion, and smell, and they forget their home phone numbers a lot as well. They may be found years later, wearing the same pair of motley leggings they donned a week post-partum, shrugging their shoulders helplessly when asked where they've been all this time. Other people take to parenting with religious zeal, turning eventually into the dread Parent Police, as fanatic in their child-rearing beliefs as the Taliban, and about as willing to accost you in the street for your own infidel ways.

Back before you yourself were a parent, you might have noticed how loony parents were, if you noticed them at all (one of the reasons nonparents avoid parents like a bad flu bug). But now that you've joined their ranks, you can see what the problem is. It's upbringing. No matter how much you object to how your own mom and dad raised you, that's the only model you

♡ ♡ ♡ ♡ ♡ ♡ ♡ ♡ ♡ ♡ ♡ ♡ ♡ ♡ ♡ ♡ ♡ ♡

THE SIX KINDS OF PARENTS

TEENAGE PARENTS. Depressingly young. May be your age by the time their baby is eighteen. Haven't read any of the literature. Don't know who Dr. Spock is, much less T. Berry Brazelton or Penelope Leach, but baby seems to be thriving anyway. Make your money worries seem petty. Mom, who sports a navel ring, doesn't look like she just had a baby. Make you feel grateful for your college years but also very old.

RICH PARENTS. Hard to find since the person out with the baby is usually the nanny. If you do spy the mother, she may look tanned and rested, with a brow unfurrowed by the usual worries that befall new parents. Sport very expensive equipment, including some Italian accessories you've never seen before. Not a lot to talk about unless asking for a stock tip or tennis instructor.

♡ ♡ ♡ ♡ ♡ ♡ ♡ ♡ ♡ ♡ ♡ ♡ ♡ ♡ ♡ ♡ ♡ ♡

♡ ♡ ♡ ♡ ♡ ♡ ♡ ♡ ♡ ♡ ♡ ♡ ♡ ♡ ♡ ♡ ♡ ♡

GRANOLA PARENTS. Cotton diapers, of course. And baby clothes that are hand-stitched from 100-percent organic hemp fibers by indigenous Indian women. The child will be breast fed until he's five years old, after which Mom will grow her own organic food and grind it herself into puree with a mortar and pestle. Make you feel very plastic and guilty.

OLDER PARENTS. Frequently mistaken for grandparents on first sighting (although they're too smartly dressed). They waited until the very last minute to have their child and are now looking ten years older due to stress and lack of sleep and loss of control over their previously well-ordered lives. Usually have subscriptions to all the professional child development and pediatric psychology journals. May be pushing a triplet stroller.

COMPETITIVE PARENTS. Have a child who uttered its first word at two months and by six months has written his first sonata. Their baby is gifted. Big for his age. Off the charts in weight and height, and now has a vocabulary of 250 words in English and 182 in Spanish. At nine months is enrolled in French, violin, and tennis lessons, and is, in case you were wondering, on the waiting list for the kindergarten that is a feeder school for Harvard . . .

PARENTS LIKE YOU. True believers.

♡ ♡ ♡ ♡ ♡ ♡ ♡ ♡ ♡ ♡ ♡ ♡ ♡ ♡ ♡ ♡ ♡ ♡

have to go by when it comes time to raise your own kid. So *their* way, give and take a little fine tuning—no cross-country family car trips to Yosemite, for example—is generally *your* way. And you'll probably change your mind about Yosemite before the kid is out of grade school. The bottom line is this: we all turn into our parents, whether we intend to or not.

This means that on top of everybody's normal neuroses are the neuroses of their parents, and their parents' parents, and so on, so that everyone is a quivering emotional mess by the time they bring their own children into the world, and it's that much harder to leave the house each morning, much less make new friends. Still, you're compelled to try, if only to find a few other people who won't begrudge you the need to be in bed by 9 P.M.

So where does one meet other members of the tribe? They're everywhere—you've just never noticed them before. Until you're a parent yourself, the people carrying infants in front-packs or pushing them along in strollers are all but invisible to you. But now you can't walk down the street without counting five or six strollers. Suddenly you spy babies in front-packs peeking out from the coats and sweaters of every third person you pass. You may also be in contact with people you met in your Lamaze class, if you had enough foresight and brain cells available to have taken down their numbers and not lost them yet. Chances are these people became parents at about the same time as you, which automatically puts them in the running as new-parent friends.

Otherwise, you must start by going to the places parents go. As a rule, these are not the places you used to frequent—the nice restaurants, the new plays, the movie theaters. Parents, and especially brand-new parents, tend to avoid these places. Instead, they congregate in the places generally shunned by the nonparent population—playgrounds, zoos, toy stores. You'll have to begin hanging out in these places if you want to meet any of your own kind. Don't forget to bring baby, either, as she's the main icebreaker.

Anyone pushing a stroller is fair game. All you have to do is meet their eyes and smile at them. My rule of thumb is that if they don't smile back, and lots won't, they're toast. If they do smile back, however, you may be on your way to a long and fruitful relationship. Take it to the next level and compliment their baby. Then try one of these next standard options for getting a parent relationship off the ground:

"Look at those eyes!"

"How old is that cutie?"

"Oooh! Big for his/her age!"

"Where did you have him?" (The ideal lead-in to labor horror stories.)

Or comment on their equipment: "I almost got that kind of stroller. How do you like it?"

You can thus determine the age and sex of the baby in question, as well as the financial standing of the parents holding it.

The first half hour of conversation with a potential new-parent friend is more a mutual sniffing than anything else. You've both answered the mating call and now you are sizing each other up. You're finding out each other's basic child-raising philosophies, educational status, and where you live in proximity to each other. All very important information if this relationship is going to go any further. It's also a loony-barometer. I once tried to start a conversation with another new mom in a park by using a standard, empty opener, which I thought was universally understood as a compliment: "Hey, what a big guy you've got there! He's gonna be a rugby player, I'll bet!" She shot me a dirty look and launched into a tirade about gender stereotypes and how her son was going to be a computer genius, not a rugby player, thank you. "I really hate it when people start making assumptions based on size," she said. Obviously I couldn't have this woman in my house for coffee.

Also important in this mutual sniffing is finding out what tax bracket these potential new friends fall into. Money woes are a large part of becoming a parent (although it's all relative). It's no fun hanging out with people whose idea of financial worries is whether to pay for preinstalled child car seats in the Mercedes SUV when your worries include whether you can afford a bus pass this month. Even if there's nothing else to talk about, my mom friend Mata and I can happily bitch about our impending financial ruin for hours.

Need more quick hints to determine compatibility? Here are several ways to size up potential new-parent soulmates within minutes of making initial contact:

☼ **What's their baby's name?** People who name their kids Tifani, Jordan, or Skylar generally do not mix well with parents who name theirs Sarah, William, and Miles III. Generally speaking, you won't have much in common with people who've named their kid after a Teenage Mutant Ninja Turtle when you've named yours after seven generations of Norwegian womenfolk.

☼ **Their baby's clothes.** Very soon in the game all parents begin to dress baby like they used to dress themselves, and the results are very telling. Is their little darling done up like a wedding cake or clad in mismatched separates? Unless you're a fashion hound yourself, you might want to pause before striking up a conversation with the mom and dad who've dressed their new baby in Ralph Lauren for babies. On the other hand, if their tot is wearing a baby-size version of your favorite football team's jersey, the segue into friendly banter is made that much easier.

☼ **Strollers.** Purists out there can divide the world into two kinds of parents: those who buy $350 Peg Perago prams and those who make do with the $14 Kmart umbrella stroller specials. The many shades in-between can be just as telling, however. If these parents live locally, they're apt to have their stroller strung with all manner of shopping bags. If they're fastidiously neat, their stroller will be pristine—the sign of a thorough and anal cleaning after every use. If they have a twin stroller, do they have a second, older child running amok or are we talking fertility drugs? Look closely and make your move accordingly.

☼ **Percentile dropping.** Some new moms, upon first meeting, cannot keep themselves from telling you where on the percentile chart their baby is in relation to all other mere children. If you're like-minded, this is a match made in heaven (especially if your children stay head-to-head on that percentile chart). Conversely, if you don't give a damn about how big your child's head circumference is in relation to his peers, you can avoid this mom in the future.

Tragically, however, new-parent friends are a transient lot. The nesting instinct hits a couple hard within the first year of having a new baby, and the lure of family, affordable housing, and a sense of community all become too strong to resist. People move back to their hometowns—the very ones they fled in disgust fifteen years earlier—in droves. If you live in a transient town like San Francisco, where I live, within a year of giving birth you can expect to lose up to 80 percent of the friendly couples you met in your Lamaze class. Another 15 percent stay in town but morph into a parental type you can't stand. The remaining 5 percent are the pool from which you must choose your new-parent friends. Pray that you actually meet each other one day.

A Friend in Pees . . .

Thea and I met at Lamaze. She and her husband sat next to me and my husband, and as part of a "getting to know you" exercise, we got to interview each other.

♡ ♡ ♡ ♡ ♡ ♡ ♡ ♡ ♡ ♡ ♡ ♡ ♡ ♡ ♡ ♡ ♡ ♡ ♡ ♡

Inspector Gadget

(New Stuff You'll Be Wanting Right About Now)

By three months your baby is starting to look a lot more like your original idea of a baby, and less like the alarming red, screaming chicken you actually birthed. He's actually doing things, too, like looking at you, smiling, cooing, and waving his adorable little fists in the air. Time to get a whole bunch of new stuff to encourage and cultivate further tricks.

When baby can hold his head up confidently (around two months), he's old enough to be carted around in a **FRONT-PACK** (also known as a Snugli). These things will set you back almost a whole Franklin, and you need a Ph.D. in physics to figure out how to strap them on right. But they can mean the difference between productivity and nonproductivity, especially if your baby doesn't like to be set down ever. You can get a lot done with a baby strapped to your front, including the laundry, the dishes, the grocery

♡ ♡ ♡ ♡ ♡ ♡ ♡ ♡ ♡ ♡ ♡ ♡ ♡ ♡ ♡ ♡ ♡ ♡ ♡ ♡

♡ ♡ ♡ ♡ ♡ ♡ ♡ ♡ ♡ ♡ ♡ ♡ ♡ ♡ ♡ ♡ ♡ ♡ ♡

shopping, and the dogs walked. Of course, you may develop a severe back problem, but that's a small price to pay. Several months later you can get a **BABY BACKPACK**. These are also expensive, but make a good alternative to a gym membership. The most effective method of using a baby backpack is to make Dad wear it.

A lot of families swear by **BABY SWINGS**, which can soothe the savage colic monster like nothing else. Or strap him in a **BOUNCY CHAIR** and let him bounce. The best invention ever for keeping baby occupied yet safely constrained in the bathroom while you take a shower.

Now that they've stopped making baby-walkers (now deemed evil and dangerous, especially in the hands of people stupid enough to put one anywhere near a staircase), your option these days is to buy one of those garish **EXER-ROCKER** things for your living room. They're stationary save for a bouncy option.

Oh, ok. Go ahead and buy one of those red, black, and white things for baby, a.k.a. an **ACTIVITY MAT**. He may actually get something out of it, and you'll get to sit and watch him kick and scream happily for at least half an hour.

And do buy a **CAMCORDER**, because you WILL be looking back on all of this—as early as next year—and laughing.

♡ ♡ ♡ ♡ ♡ ♡ ♡ ♡ ♡ ♡ ♡ ♡ ♡ ♡ ♡ ♡ ♡ ♡ ♡

They were both former actors. She was a jeweler, and he now managed the advertising department of a local alternative newspaper. They were funny, self-effacing, literate, and terrified of what life with a baby would be like. We bonded instantly.

And good thing, too. Because throughout those first few months we needed to walk each other through life as we now knew it. Turns out our own moms, God bless them, couldn't quite recall the details of our own bouts with colic or colds thirty-some years ago. And the baby books just weren't as personal as we'd like. So Thea and I memorized each other's numbers and called to check in every day in that first, sleep-deprived month. We compared notes and bounced ideas off each other, sifting through the various expert opinions and doling out family wisdom. We weren't so much comparing babies as making sure they were both on the same sort of track. "How many times do you have to feed her during the night? Has she smiled yet? No? Good, mine neither."

We relied upon each other utterly. She could call me in a panic any time day or night (chances are I'd be up, anyway), and I'd do my best to reassure her, or give her the second opinion she needed to feel justified in bothering the pediatric nurse hot line attendants one more time. Mentally, we occupied the same blank, gray space of new mothers everywhere: our hormones crashing, our body clocks broken, our vocabularies a third of their former selves. We'd take our newborns to the park and sit there happily, secure in the knowledge that, even if the other did have something intelligent to say, she wouldn't be able to articulate it.

Then one evening she called up. "I've got some bad news," she said, and my head began to sway. Something happened to her daughter. Something happened to her husband. Car crash? Cancer? Nuclear war? Worse.

"We're moving back East," she said.

Oh no.

Oh, I won't bore you with details, but he got a job offer he couldn't refuse, so good, in fact, that they were actually going to be able to buy a house. A real house, with a picket fence and a living tree in front. What was I going to say to stop them? But San Francisco's so . . . pretty?

I would never find another mom as mellow and friendly as Thea.

But miraculously, I did. I met Trisha at a local video store with her daughter, Maggie, who looked to be the same age as Annie. I smiled. She smiled. She made the next move with the standard opener: "What a cutie. How old is she?"

We quickly exchanged phone numbers. When we met up the next week, we spent three full hours gathering each other's vital statistics: How long was your labor? Epidural or not? How was your OB? Breast feeding? Bottle? Her husband and my husband got along famously, as well. Sometimes we'd go to their apartment, and our husbands would sit with their daughters in their laps and talk about favorite pop bands or football scores. We were all in the same tax bracket, all lived in one-bedroom apartments, all wondered how we were going to afford something bigger in this town that had suddenly, thanks to the Internet Gold Rush, become the land of $400,000 starter homes.

The answer to that quandary came to them just a few months later. Bob, a cook, got a job offer from his previous employer back in Boston for a much higher rank and a much fatter paycheck. This, combined with their families clamoring for them to return with their little one, and the fact that one can rent a house outside of Boston for the price of an unimpressive one-bedroom apartment here, made the decision a no-brainer. They moved back within the month. Wave bye-bye.

Understandably, then, the very first thing I asked Meg upon meeting her in Golden Gate Park and sensing a meeting of minds, was not "How bad was your labor?" but "Are you planning on moving back East anytime soon?"

No way, said she. She was a California native. She had nowhere else to go.

THE BAWL AND CHAIN

Within a couple of months of settling on Planet Parenthood, you become aware of a few inalienable truths, the facts of your new life. Key among these truths is the grinding monotony that has replaced what was once, at least as you remember it, a wildly exciting, carefree lifestyle. This new reality begins settling in early, soon after the sleep deprivation has worn off but long before baby needs shoes. By three months or

so, baby has developed her own little schedule of feedings, naps, playtimes, fussy times, more feedings, and
more naps, and it is you, her parents, who are falling
into line with it. You find yourselves passing on invita-
tions to dinner at a friend's house because it conflicts
with baby's storytime. Your plans to check out a bigger
apartment this afternoon are thwarted because baby
hasn't wakened from her nap yet. Here again all your
worst stereotypes about parenthood are coming up hor-
ribly true—there's a real ball and chain operation
going on here, and it's got nothing to do with your
spouse.

"Parenthood is one long exercise
 in losing your ideals."
   —JOAN, MOTHER OF TWO

But babies demand a schedule. And true, after the
trauma of the first three months is over, both of you are
honestly grateful for that schedule. It at least means
that now you know you can watch "Melrose Place" reruns uninterrupted after dinner and before baby wakes
up for her 10 P.M. feeding. It means you know she'll
wake up at 2-ish, 5-ish, and 7-ish for additional feedings, and you can live with that, as long as they are di-
vided up fairly between the two of you. You know you
can have your cup of coffee and read the headlines
when baby goes down for her first nap at 9 A.M., and
you can gird your loins for the daily 5 P.M. meltdown. It

can be a perfectly acceptable little life for the three of you.

Still, the completeness of this agreement, the utter non-negotiableness of it, can be a shock to some formerly jet-setting sorts, who maybe thought they were signing up for the cute bubbly progeny package that seemingly goes home with the nanny when she leaves at 6 P.M. each night.

Seasoned parents have either resigned themselves to this new fact of life, or they've developed crafty tricks for getting around it. Some examples:

☼ You can still go out with friends—providing they come over and bring the pizza.

☼ Surround yourself with new-parent friends, who understand that dinner has to be over by six so you can put baby down by seven and fall into bed yourself by nine, and who won't laugh at you for this standard.

☼ One word: VCR

☼ Take turns experiencing refreshing draughts of total freedom. Offer to do all off-site chores as long as the other watches the baby while you're doing them.

☼ Learn to love parks, zoos, and aquariums. Reacquaint yourselves with the backyard outing, Sunday dinner with Grandma, long stroller walks to nowhere in particular.

☀ Stop thinking about it for the next fourteen years.

SEX? (seks) n. [L. sexus] 1. Either of the two divisions of organisms distinguished as male and female 2. The character of being male or female 3. The attraction between the sexes 4. Sexual intercourse

If you're new parents, I thought the above definition might help.

Whenever I read about women who have children less than a year apart, I can only shake my head in wonder and give a little shudder. Forget the logistical nightmare they've made for themselves, it's the math that horrifies me: *They HAD SEX that soon after birth?!*

Any woman who had a vaginal birth knows what I'm talking about. It's really quite remarkable that millions of years of evolution haven't come up with a better way to get a seven-pound baby out of you than through that one, none-too-large orifice. At the end of the day, your poor, traumatized yoni has been battered, bruised, stretched beyond recognition, and probably even cut and stitched back together to boot. In the first six weeks postpartum, standing up is a whole new sensation, as is sitting down, squatting, kneeling, or maintaining any position that isn't horizontal with your feet on a pillow. One of the best pieces of secret birthing wisdom my cousin gave me before I went into labor was "take a package of laxatives with you to the hospital, just in case." It was good advice. (If you need to be told why, you must not have had your baby yet . . .) The books all say you can start having sex again after six weeks, but for most women, the very idea makes them faint.

While the damage to your tender female organs was being done, your man, in this day and age, anyway, got the privilege of standing there and watching it. Being the visually aroused creatures they are, the memory of this ordeal lingers for months and kills any thought of sex, with *you* at least.

Some men may already be retrained for this new, sex-free relationship, especially if they or their mates were turned off by the pregnancy. By the time the baby is born, men in this camp have already rechanneled their sexual energies into other venues, such as golf or the Playboy Channel. However, for those men who were wildly turned on by their women's full, fertile bodies, and whose mates turned into nymphos during pregnancy (all that blood circulating down there, you know), the sudden shutdown of their sex lives can be traumatizing.

Every couple is different, of course, but judging from the literature and a highly unscientific survey of all my new-parent friends, it's fairly clear that once baby is born, the days of hot, romping, full-body sex are over for a good long while. What replaces it is a sort of quick, grudging, economy-package sex that relieves the tension and makes you remember for a few moments what sex was like back when you first met each other and had nothing but time and privacy on your hands.

Whole books have been written about the many reasons why your sex life goes south after the birth of a baby. It certainly seems like a good topic. But as any seasoned parent unmuddled by advanced psychology degrees can tell you, it all boils down to three things: exhaustion, less privacy, and new and alarming self-image problems for both Mom and Dad.

Fortunately, sex is the furthest thing from everyone's minds in the first month after childbirth. Both of you are far too shell-shocked to be waxing passionate, and the new mom is doubtless in some form of pain, be it her stitches or her cesarean or her hemorrhoids. The new dad is just trying to get through the day on half an hour of sleep, with a squalling infant next to the bed and a sobbing, hysterical wife. When you do have a moment to get horizontal, you use it for deep, heavy sleeping, thank you.

Later on, however, usually sometime after the third month when things have settled down as much as they're going to, the two of you begin to realize that your marital relationship now consists exclusively of a smooch and maybe a caress before falling into a deep, comalike sleep each night. Both of you realize that this sad state of affairs shouldn't stand. But only one of you can summon the energy to do anything about it. And here's a hint: it isn't the person who actually birthed the baby.

Apart from the few males who start thinking of their wives as "Mother" (note the capital M) and stop bringing up the topic of sex altogether, most men, be-ing men, seem ready to rumble a few weeks postpartum. For obvious reasons they don't seem to suffer from the same total exhaustion as women, nor do they appear to care whether baby can hear you or not. They just wanna do it.

Women, however, take a while longer to warm back up. For a lot of new mothers, sex occupies a space deep down on the list of things to do with any spare time, falling long after such options as sleeping, reading a magazine article in one sitting, taking a hot bath, doing a load of laundry, or plowing the back forty.

Why is this? Pick your reason. Maybe it's your new, fully utilitarian body that's keeping you from donning the negligee anew. If you're still breast feeding and have tried to get down with your man, you will probably have experienced a rather embarrassing byproduct of lactation that nobody mentions until it's too late: Fountain Tits. It seems sexual arousal stimulates the same hormones that affect the let-down reflex, so you suddenly find yourself engaged in kinky waterworks when all you intended was standard-issue woman-on-top. Your man may love being covered in breast milk, or he may not, and you may think it's hot or you may be horrified. Either way, unless you both have lactation fetishes, this new twist can definitely dampen the mood.

It may be the ten or more pounds on your butt or hips or thighs that haven't melted away yet, as promised. Again, your husband may not care, but then again he might. In any case he'd be wise to keep his mouth shut on this matter in particular. Your body has just been through nine months of pregnancy, then labor, then zero sleep plus possibly an infant who is eating you alive every two to three hours. You've been put through the wringer, and Dad, bless his little balding head, has not. You may not feel as comfortable dancing around naked as you once did, but do you really have to justify it at the moment?

Or maybe you feel far more motherly now than sexy. Can you picture your own mother having sex? Don't really want to? Maybe that's part of the problem now. You feel like a mom and no longer like that vixen of two years ago who danced on tabletops in a slinky black numbah cut down to there. The metamorphosis into a mother is the most radical change in a woman's life, even if she thought she was ready for it. The transformation is a lot more sudden and complete for women than it is for men, who generally meander into fatherhood, and for whom it's more a state of mind than of body. How can you be a frivolous, flirtatious girl anymore when your every cell is bent on feeding and protecting the fruit of your womb? How can you be expected to do the nasty when you're 200-percent preoccupied with something else? Of course, some women never have this problem, and have no difficulties maintaining a sex drive with a baby on their hip. Others snap out of it within a year. Those of us with daughters suddenly realize we'll need to come up with a plausible explanation for our single, pre-Dad days in about fifteen short years.

And let's not forget privacy, which, like butt thongs and long, quiet evenings spent by the fire, is a thing of your previous lives. Just because your infant can't climb out of his crib yet doesn't mean you have the kind of privacy you had back in the old days when only the dog could hear your cries of passion. The biggest question for new parents after their sex life has resumed (such as it has) is this: How long can we do this before we traumatize the baby? You know when to expect baby's first smile, first tooth, and first step, but when can a baby start to decipher certain bumps and groans in the night? Will you scar him for life if he sees the two of you exchanging saliva?

Even when the planets line up and both of you are feeling frisky, the baby is napping in the other room, and there's no other competing interest in sight, the chances of taking yourselves all the way to a pleasurable and long-forgotten conclusion are slim. "Nothing kills an erection faster than a baby's cry." Somebody, somewhere, once said that, and whether it was your husband or your grandfather hardly matters. It was true one hundred years ago just as it holds true now.

Sex as parents takes on the furtiveness of sex as teenagers. In stark contrast to your prechild lives, you start locking the door to your bedroom, even before your baby is mobile—just in case. You have quickies in the bathroom. You hide underneath the blankets and try to keep as quiet as possible. It never gets any easier. Once your child is a walking, talking toddler, even these techniques won't work. Try to kiss each other in the kitchen and any normal two-and-a-half-year-old will run up and push you apart, scolding, "No Daddy! No Mommy!" And you'll guiltily oblige, wondering how much he knows.

Alas, this is the state of sex in your first year of parenthood. The women's magazines can't help you. The Penthouse Letters can serve a particular purpose, but mostly they just depress you. My best suggestion is the most hackneyed—but a proven result-getter. You must get Grandma to come stay with junior for a three-day weekend while the two of you go somewhere—even the Motel 6 downtown. It doesn't have to be fancy as long as it's away from home.

Use the first day to sleep and sleep only. Sleep late, get breakfast, go back to your room, and take a nap. Have lunch and then have another nap. Get to bed by eight that night and sleep as late as you want into Day Two. Guaranteed, your outlook will be much improved, and you may even be up for a little morning (or early afternoon, depending on how long you slept in) nookie. Spend Day Two doing whatever datelike activity you once so enjoyed. Eat at a nice restaurant. Don't skimp on the wine. Back at the motel, throw your clothes in the corner and trash the bed. Make porno movie noises. At about 11 P.M. order room service and a dirty movie. Continue as before. The next morning you will wake up happy and rested and basking in that glow you felt when you first fell in love. Take a shower together, then get breakfast, take a deep breath, and rush home to see your little guy, whom you'll be missing by now. Finally, make a date to do this again in six months.

PARENTAL CHIC

Now that you've become a bona fide parent, you might as well look the part. The first thing you'll need to do is rid your closet of all fine silks, expensive leathers, imported linens, light-colored clothing, and anything that needs to be dry-cleaned. Next, give away everything that you can't throw on the floor or hang in the bathroom.

You'll notice that leaves jeans, sweatshirts, shorts, and leggings. This is your new-parent uniform. Learn to love it, since you'll be wearing a version of it for many years to come. This goes for women and men, who typically gain a good ten pounds in solidarity with their wives. My suggestion for new moms is to not bother trying to fit into your prepartum jeans at all and just run out and buy a couple pairs of pants two sizes larger. No sense looking sloppy AND fat.

It will be best if you just forget about looking hip for the next twenty years, since it simply can't be done if you're out in public with your child. All the leather in the world can't counter the impact of a cute little baby wrapped up in pastel colors on your person. In San Francisco, where I live, you often see people who haven't learned this lesson, folks who are multipierced, dressed in all-black Goth attire, or sporting magenta hair. That look is foiled every time by the ducky-yellow stroller they're pushing, or that powder-blue baby backpack.

Not that style or fashion will be an important part of your life anymore. The time it took you to put to-

♡ ♡ ♡ ♡ ♡ ♡ ♡ ♡ ♡ ♡ ♡ ♡ ♡ ♡ ♡ ♡ ♡

THE BABY WORKOUT

Just accept this fact: Unless you're seventeen years old, your body will never be exactly the same as it was prebaby, and no woman should waste precious moments when she could be sleeping worrying about it. We've all read stories in *People* about the stars who've managed to slim back down quickly after childbirth. And if you can pay for a twenty-four-hour professional nanny, a dietitian, a cook, and a personal trainer, you can probably do the same. For the rest of us, however, the hip huggers are a thing of the past.

However, nature provides for the new mom by sneakily giving her strength like she's never known before. A baby is the ideal form of weight training because it adds pounds slowly, starting low and daily adding ounces, so you never realize you're working out until you're shocked at the size of your biceps. Here are some other areas of the body that benefit from the Baby Workout:

☼ PECTORALS. Gain strength by holding your ever-growing baby out in front of you for others to hold. Repeat as often as necessary.

☼ FOREARM TENDON. Nothing besides waitressing builds up your forearm like manually pumping breast

♡ ♡ ♡ ♡ ♡ ♡ ♡ ♡ ♡ ♡ ♡ ♡ ♡ ♡ ♡ ♡ ♡

♡ ♡ ♡ ♡ ♡ ♡ ♡ ♡ ♡ ♡ ♡ ♡ ♡ ♡ ♡ ♡ ♡

milk. If you're expressing milk at all, you have to pump four or five times a day, creating the condition known as "Popeye Forearm."

☀ LOWER BACK. Slow in coming, but after the pain of constantly bending over to pick up and put down baby subsides, you'll eventually build the back strength of a yogi.

☀ THIGHS. Thighs of steel come from constantly dropping things because your hands are full these days. Ordinarily, you'd bend over, but now you've got an infant to hold, so you squat, back straight, and let your thighs hoist you back up. Thighs of steel will come in handy when pushing your stroller up hills.

☀ HIPS. After baby is old enough to cling to your hip, it's the handiest place to keep him, enabling you to work your hip, stomach, and bicep muscles as you go about your day. Works along the same lines as Pilates, but cheaper.

☀ FULL BODY. "The All-Body Schlepp" is a mysterious new ability to carry twice as much on your person than at any other time in your life. Schlepping helps you get baby, stroller, diaper bag, extra toys, camera, purse, and two whole bags of groceries to the car in one trip. Makes it possible to continue using public transportation. Builds stamina and determination, along with a sense of the absurd.

♡ ♡ ♡ ♡ ♡ ♡ ♡ ♡ ♡ ♡ ♡ ♡ ♡ ♡ ♡ ♡ ♡

gether a suitable ensemble for public consumption before the birth of your baby is now taken up by trying to get baby ready for public viewing. Nor is that average 3.5 hours of sleep you're working on doing much for your sense of style. In the first months after your baby's birth, your biggest challenge will be to get clothes *on*, not to look good in them.

My friend Christina remembers the days she used to hit late-night poetry readings in New York City wearing nothing but tight, worn 501s and a package of Marlboro Lights. The comparison with what she wears now, she says, is too glaring to contemplate. She recently sat in a local park interviewing a prospective baby-sitter and realized the college girl looked a lot like her, prechildren. "I had on a brown sweater, a stained pair of blue leggings, white socks, and tennis shoes," she told me. "I could read this girl's mind. She was thinking that I was just your standard housewife . . . because that's what I'd think if I saw someone like me!" We parents, however, never pass judgments like these. We know how hard it was to find clean socks.

There will be exceptions. There are always exceptions. If you've ventured outside at all, you've probably run across a mom or dad with a baby the same age as yours who looks as if she or he is dressed for a shareholder's meeting. These people clearly have valets or other hired help to assist them in getting out the door in the morning and probably don't even handle their own children. These kinds of people are not representative of new parents in general, and you are allowed to ignore them. Better still, feel free to hang back and watch them for the inevitable accident, and guffaw loudly when their little prince or princess leaves a big pee-pee stain on their tailored silk pants. Parenting is a job you have to dress for.

Concentrate instead on finding one pair of jeans that fit, one T-shirt with minimum staining (it doesn't have to match), and some form of comfortable, flat footwear. A really big sweatshirt can help pull this look together and make nonparents think you're just out for a casual day on the boat or some such. Other parents, however, will not be fooled.

For Mom and Dad, then, the new look is all about comfort, convenience, and what can best be stored and pulled from the hamper five out of seven days a week. (Weekends are easy because you can generally wear what you slept in.)

New parents almost universally put more energy into dressing their progeny than themselves. Actually, you can almost always judge how people dressed prechild by looking at the child. Some people deck their two-month-olds in Baby Dior or Ralph Lauren for babies. They'll put them in voluminous velvet dresses and wrap their bald heads with elastic beaded headbands. You'll see babies in miniature leather cowboy boots or 0–3-month-size Tommy Hilfiger parkas. DKNY recently launched an infant/toddler line directed at the more-money-than-sense set ($44 for a onesie the child will grow out of in twenty-one days?).

Shopping for baby will completely replace your urge

to shop for yourself. Even though it may not constitute dollar savings, it does represent a moral victory since you're shopping for somebody else. Baby needs clothes, right? You might feel guilty dropping $80 on yourselves these days, but $80 at Baby Gap? It's all too easy.

Just as well, anyway. You'll be bonding closely with several items of clothing—your sweatpants, your shorts, one or two T-shirts—and to these you'll stay true for the next many years. Yes, they'll get ratty, but they're comfortable. Cleanliness hardly matters to you anymore, anyway. It's just too much damn trouble. And besides, everything you own is stained. Spit-up stains. Vomit stains. Breast milk and formula both stain. Don't bother hoping baby will grow out of this secretion stage, because when he does he will go straight into toddler mode and trash your house as well as your wardrobe.

Well, don't you look a sight? I can see you're breaking in. You're holding up nicely, both of you. Keep reminding yourselves that the things that don't kill you make you stronger. At any rate, things are going to be getting a little easier in the next few months. Or at least a little more pleasant to be around.

chapter 4

THE KODAK MONTHS

(6–8 Months)

"Even when freshly washed and relieved of all obvious confections, children tend to be sticky."

—FRAN LEBOWITZ

Nature is no dummy. A normal baby develops as it does because the process, honed and standardized over the millennia, is perfectly designed to keep parents engaged, interested, and less likely to kill it before its first birthday. Babies start smiling at around six weeks because at one point in evolution all the babies who didn't by that time were thrown out of the cave by crazed, sleep-deprived parents who were sick of caring for such an unresponsive beast. At three months they're cooing and doing their cute little kicks and urps so that the adults in their lives are once again made interested and pick them up to play. At six months, babies are at the peak of their baby cuteness and are starting to develop an actual personality. By eight months they're enchanting little people—laughing, happy little Buddhist monks, but without the saffron robes or celebrity hangers-on. Everyone wants to be with baby now, even people who want nothing to do with babies. When people talk about wanting to "eat that baby up," they're talking about the Kodak Months.

USEFUL TERMS

A "HIGH-NEEDS" CHILD A screamer. A colicky kid. A baby you pray is a friend's and not your own.

A "SPIRITED" CHILD Ditto. A screamer.

MOMMY AND ME A kind of class you can enroll your baby in as an excuse to get out of the house and meet other mommies and compare children.

PERCENTILE As in, <u>my</u> child is in the 95th percentile for weight. Where's yours? This refers to the chart pediatricians keep to monitor your child's growth. It's not supposed to be competitive, but in this day and age, naturally it is.

PLAY DATES, PLAY GROUPS In our parent's era, these were known as "the neighborhood" and "the neighborhood kids."

♡ ♡ ♡ ♡ ♡ ♡ ♡ ♡ ♡ ♡ ♡ ♡ ♡ ♡ ♡ ♡ ♡

By now, you new parents may think you've gotten everything down, but in reality you're only halfway there. You're not quite a fully-vested citizen of Planet Parenthood, with voting rights and parking privileges. Oh, no. The first year brings surprises and unforeseen twists at every turn. You're never a pro at parenting in the first year unless you're talking to parents with first babies younger than yours. And you're only on equal footing with Grandma after you've successfully raised and launched as many chillens as she has. Just remember: beauty has its price. And you're soon to get a look at that price tag. In the meantime, keep your mouth shut and stay humble.

JEEPERS, CREEPERS

You might say that crawling is the accomplishment that separates the infants from the babies. Until they start crawling, infants are totally dependent on you for everything. You take them from Point A to Point B when you want and not before. But one day you'll look up from your paper and notice that baby is no longer on his baby blanket on the floor, where you left him, but in the hallway and headed for the door. This is an alarming new development. Your baby is suddenly mobile, and it means a whole new world of anxiety for both of you. Baby suddenly becomes fixated on escape, and your job becomes foiling that escape.

Crawling is a long time coming for most babies (except, of course, the Gifted Ones). The first sign that they're prepping to start trying is when they can sit up by themselves, usually by five to six months. You'll prop them up on their little baby blankets in the middle of the floor, and they'll survey the room with a gleam in their eye. The daring among them will then begin to devise ways of mobilization. This is another period when you're very glad you bowed to temptation and bought a camcorder. Baby will spend several months in various machinations of motion: she'll twitch on her belly, pull herself along like G.I. Jane, or hump along like a sea lion on the beach. Some will stay on their hands and knees all day, rocking to and fro like idling economy cars. A lot of babies finally get the hang of crawling but not the concept of *forward* for another month, giving you many opportunities to rescue them from underneath the couch or dining room chairs. Some babies create new and unusual forms of forward momentum that bear little resemblance to what you think of as crawling. My friend Mata's daughter, Isabelle, propelled herself quite agilely by scooting along on her butt and one bent leg, like a hermit crab. It was funny looking yet effective. Other babies never get around to crawling at all.

I met a woman at the park whose daughter, at ten months, didn't crawl. The baby would sit on the ground and reach desperately for the toys in front of her, but for some reason she couldn't pull off the necessary physical machinations to get herself to them. Her parents, very easygoing, nonhysterical types, were working up to some serious, high-grade panic, spending their nights surfing the Internet for, and their days getting on the waiting lists of, various developmental specialists. Then, mere minutes before they were going to admit to fellow parents that something was definitely wrong with their girl,

♡ ♡ ♡ ♡ ♡ ♡ ♡ ♡ ♡ ♡ ♡ ♡ ♡ ♡ ♡ ♡ ♡ ♡

WHAT YOU'LL NEED IN THE KODAK MONTHS

☼ **BABY GATES.** Because now that he can reach the brink, you don't want him jumping.

☼ **BABY UTENSILS, BABY BOWLS, BABY CUPS.** Finally you can dust off these items, which you probably got by the dozens six months ago. But keep one word firmly in mind: plastic.

☼ **BIBS.** Now that baby is teething in earnest, you need something to blot the drool. Bibs are the one fashion accessory you cannot live without during the Kodak months.

☼ **FILM.** And lots of it. Indoor/outdoor 35mm film for your camera, which should be ever-present, just in case. And lots of tapes for your camcorder.

What you won't need:

☼ **BABY KNEE-PADS.** Yeah, I know these might seem like a good idea at first, but just because <u>you</u> can't spend all day on your knees without serious injury doesn't mean your baby can't. Besides, these will just impede his progress toward expert crawling, and piss him off in the process. And you don't want that.

♡ ♡ ♡ ♡ ♡ ♡ ♡ ♡ ♡ ♡ ♡ ♡ ♡ ♡ ♡ ♡ ♡ ♡

she stood up. She was eleven months old, and had apparently decided to give the whole crawling thing a miss.

"This probably means she'll be a perfect teenager and wait until she's twenty before she shaves her head and joins a cult," her much relieved dad told me later. At least he didn't have to explain her at the park anymore.

However your baby decides to do it, crawling gets you big frequent flier miles toward Planet Parenthood. Now your baby can actively move away from you and appears to be doing so with gusto. Try not to let your feelings get hurt; it's nothing personal. In the meantime, you're about to enter a new and more challenging phase of parenthood—parenting the mobile unit. Before you know it, baby will be "pulling up" on everything he can find, which is sort of the equivalent of getting a learner's permit. He's not walking yet, but he's dreaming of it.

100 PERCENT BABYPROOF

The problem is, when baby gets mobile, Mom and Dad get nervous.

There's no point in "babyproofing" your abode until baby gets to this stage, unless you're planning on personally walking him over to the open window or the hot stove. After all, baby can't stick his finger in a light socket if he can't get to it yet, can he? (You should know better by now.) It's silly to babyproof the house for a two-month-old who's not going anywhere, but there's no point in waiting for ugly surprises like a finger in the socket to make your home baby-safe. When baby starts pulling up on the furniture, it's best to have everything bolted down.

You can hire a consultant to come in and tell you that your home is a death trap and every plant in your garden is highly poisonous, and that he can do the job for under a grand, but you'll have to hire somebody else for the landscaping overhaul. Or you can use your God-given common sense (assuming you have any) and do the job yourself.

First things first: kiss your tastefully designed home good-bye for the next couple of years. There can be no more beautiful potted plants within reaching distance; no more fragile objets d'art on your coffee table; no expensive rugs you can't afford to destroy (vomit/poop/milk/strained peaches don't really dry-clean out very well). Those gorgeous glass and iron side tables? Wrap 'em up and put them in the garage unless you can stand the suspense of guessing when and how bad your baby's eventual collision with them will be. You might as well wall up that fireplace, too, and save yourself the ulcer. Sure, you're babyproofing to make the house safe for a newly mobile infant, but a large part of that means putting away everything you give a damn about and leaving the dreck baby can go at with abandon.

You'll have to start learning to think like an orally fixated baby. You'll have to train yourself to pick up any coins that fall from your pocket en route to the dresser coin bottle. No more letting paper clips or staples fall where they may around your desk. For the first time in your life you'll find a button on the floor and immediately sew it back from whence it came, where it's safe. You will constantly be amazed at the amount and variety of detritus on the floors of average, cleanish homes. Dust bunnies, dead flies, kitty litter—your baby won't discriminate, so don't give him the option of a taste-test.

Next, you have to gate all your stairways so your little creeper won't find himself at the brink and decide to jump. You'll just have to get used to stepping over

♡ ♡ ♡ ♡ ♡ ♡ ♡ ♡ ♡ ♡ ♡ ♡ ♡ ♡ ♡ ♡ ♡

STANDARD DOUBLE STANDARDS

Now that you've been parents for a while, you may have noticed several glaring double standards that apply to your gender. There's nothing like having a baby to tweak all our enlightened, twenty-first-century notions of gender equality. Here are some of the more obvious areas these double standards apply:

☼ WORK. Employers love a family man. He's likely to stay put and work hard. He's a good candidate for promotion. A family woman? Two words: Mommy Track.

☼ BABY CARE. No matter how incompetent the woman, people assume she knows what she's doing in the realm of baby rearing. When men are skilled at giving baths and changing diapers, it's only because their wives must have taught them.

☼ PUBLIC LIFE. A mom can be a mom anywhere, even

♡ ♡ ♡ ♡ ♡ ♡ ♡ ♡ ♡ ♡ ♡ ♡ ♡ ♡ ♡ ♡ ♡

them for the next couple of years. It's handy for pets, anyway.

In babyproofing, there are two levels of danger. Level one is all the stuff on the floor and all the stuff that a baby can pull on top of himself off shelves or low tables. This is the level you need to address when your baby starts crawling. Level two comes when baby survives level one and grows into a walking, thinking toddler avenger bent on self-destruction. It's when he can get into the garage and into the paint thinner, or when he gets the bright idea to open the window and peer

♡ ♡ ♡ ♡ ♡ ♡ ♡ ♡ ♡ ♡ ♡ ♡ ♡ ♡ ♡ ♡ ♡

without her child. She can sit in a park and smile at other babies or strike up a conversation with another mom in the grocery store. Unless a dad has the baby strapped to his chest, he's a potential pervert, and someone to be glowered at.

☼ FAMILY LIFE. Men can devote their all to their careers, at the expense of their wives and children. When they've made it big, they can then have another wife, and more children, and devote their all to them in a second round. Women, generally speaking, can't do this.

☼ HOME LIFE. If a mom chooses to stay home with her kids, she gets to do all the housework as well. If she chooses to return to work, she still gets to do all the housework.

♡ ♡ ♡ ♡ ♡ ♡ ♡ ♡ ♡ ♡ ♡ ♡ ♡ ♡ ♡ ♡ ♡

down at whatever's two stories below. Level two is the level of locks and hidden high places. It's the level of bolting down bookcases and buying toilet clamps and putting medicine and vitamins and wine on shelves so high that you need to stand on a stool to reach them. My two-year-old has learned the lesson of elevation already. She takes her little toddler chair into the kitchen and stands on it to get into the cutlery drawer. She can also reach the Advil (which we can't afford to share). Needless to say, the cutlery is now behind a locked drawer that we can barely open ourselves. Ditto the life-sustaining Advil.

At the risk of sounding like a broken record, remember once again that all babies are different, and as such each requires a different level of babyproofing. You can babyproof your house for your particular baby perfectly, and yet when the monster from down the street comes to play he discovers dozens of ways to wreak havoc and endanger himself. If it's never occurred to your child to crawl into the toilet, rest assured it's the favorite pastime of his or her playmate. Be prepared.

You will have to mine sweep your parents' house as well since grandparents are notorious for filling the garage with toys for their grandchild . . . but leaving the Drano and lye on the bottom shelf of an unlocked storage shed.

All of this is a must if you want to survive with your peace of mind intact. You'll live easier knowing that every time your baby crawls or twaddles out of sight it isn't to pull the aquarium down onto himself. Besides, once you've developed hyperaware skills of observation and danger avoidance, you're ready to tackle the outside world with a walking-age baby, another hair-raising milestone that ages you well beyond your child-free peers.

FOOD FOR ONE

It's easy to pretend baby is not an actual human being for the first four or five months. After all, it's not as if she's interacting with you in any way, joining you for a coffee and cigarette at breakfast, and telling you her views on the latest White House scandal. In the first few months, when babies are mostly unresponsive, un-fathomable little creatures, they might as well be an exotic breed of chinchilla that you have to bottle-feed and keep warm. This might help keep total panic at bay for a few months. But it's hard to keep up such a fa-cade once baby starts smiling at you, especially with those all-body smiles that erupt whenever you bend over to play with her, and starts watching you in-tensely everywhere you go. A few months after that she starts to want solid food. And as everyone knows, you can't spoon-feed a chinchilla. What you've got here is a very rudimentary, and very hungry, human.

This presents a whole world of new problems, espe-cially if you're like me and don't know how to make anything besides takeout. Breast and bottle feeding were easy, by comparison. Up until now, you simply filled a bottle with formula up to that little eight-ounce mark, which by now you'd finally learned how to do, even in your traumatized, sleep-deprived state, and popped it into your little bird's mouth. Breast feeding involved even less skill—just lift up your shirt and lunch was ready. In neither case did you have to know anything about nutrition, or calories, or protein, or any of those other scary food questions. But around four or five months some instinct will kick in to prompt your thinking on heartier fare. *Hmm. He looks a little peckish still. And he's eyeballing my bagel. Maybe I should try to feed him real food.*

"No baby is allowed to be born unless it loves pizza."

—JEANNE MURPHY

Prepare yourself for alarmingly strong opinions on the topic, however. Feeding your offspring is probably one of the deepest primal instincts humans can still dredge up. I remember one night, about two months after having Annie, I noticed we were down to one can of formula. I was feeding her half breast milk and half formula but the latter was my fallback, and—OK I admit it—my crutch. If and when my breast milk decided to fail me, the bottle would still be full. I mentioned this to my husband, who shrugged and said he'd go to the store tomorrow and buy some more. The room suddenly got colder.

"No," I said slowly. "It might not last the night. You'd better go buy some more now."

"But it's late and it's raining," he said. "I'll go first thing in the morning, I promise."

"NO," I said, my voice rising. "We need food in this house. We need to feed Annie."

"Julie, Safeway is down the block, and it's open twenty-four hours . . . "

"WE NEED FOOD FOR OUR CHILD!"

I began to lash our sleeping infant to my body in preparation for the treacherous journey down a frozen, desolate city block, for braving the elements to reach the Safeway, where I could procure the needed provisions for my daughter and haul them back to the homestead.

I meant it, too. But Luke put on his coat instead. "I'm going, I'm going," he said, rolling his eyes. "If I'm not back in five minutes, the Indians got me. Sheesh."

So as you see, feeding your baby is one of the first conundrums you will face as a parent. First you have to decide when to start solid food, then you have to decide what to make. If you religiously adhere to whatever bulletins the American Academy of Pediatrics puts out, you won't begin your baby on solid food until six months. If you buy what most mainstream parenting books tell you, you'll begin anywhere from four to six months. If you listen to your mom, you'll start spooning the little guy watered down rice cereal at three months or earlier, since that is what they did in their day (and if you're reading this, it didn't kill you, now did it?). Grandmas say it helps a baby sleep through the night because he doesn't wake up hungry. Maybe they're right. Maybe they're not. Who knows?

Baby's not talking. So the choice is up to you. All you know is your baby seems to want more out of lunch than his milk, yet he doesn't seem up to sharing Thai takeout with you. What to do?

First of all, you'll want to go buy a requisite box of rice cereal, with that grinning Gerber baby on front. It will be in the baby food aisle of your supermarket, which for whatever reason is usually near the geriatric products and the laundry detergent, and is probably foreign territory for most of you unless you had to help raise siblings fifteen years your junior. There you will be struck dumb by the wonders of modern niche marketing. Where our mothers had a choice of green, brown, or orange puree in little jars, we can buy those same jars in three different sizes, with all organic contents, or with specially cut "second stage" food for older babies with one to three teeth. These days you can get a nosebleed pondering the giant wall of tiny jars filled with endless food combinations. Strawberry and banana, apple and squash, squash and banana, chicken and rice, rice and assorted veggies, brown rice and organic carrots. In time, your baby will let you know in no uncertain terms what constitutes acceptable menu fodder. For now, however, I recommend you go with whatever sounds good to you.

At last you'll be able to put to use all those bowl and spoon sets people gave you by the dozens, although your baby won't notice the grinning Mickey Mouse on the bottom for another year yet. Hopefully these are all plastic, because by one year your baby will have more fun flinging food than he has eating it. Start by pouring a little of the dry, flaky rice cereal into one of these bowls, and add either a little warm formula or breast milk to stir it into a palatable consistency. Put baby in his bouncy chair, cover him with a bib. Now get the camera.

"I knew I was a mom when I found myself eating random leftovers off my daughter's high chair after she'd gone to bed."

—HOLLY, MOM OF ONE

You might feel sheepish making such a big deal about baby's first food, but don't. A lot of cultures make a big deal about it. In India, they have a celebration called "First Rice," in which they smear sweet rice all over a young infant's mouth to celebrate her ongoing health and longevity. A friend of mine of Indian descent showed me the photos, prominently displayed in his parents' bedroom, of his and his sisters' first rice ceremonies. Western grandmothers have been known to take detailed video footage of this event and subject anyone they can to forced repeated viewings.

It's a big deal for baby, too. Watch his eyes as you spoon that first tiny bit of gruel into his little bud mouth. You can almost see the gears working in his head. First he'll seem surprised at this strange new texture in his mouth. Then he'll think about it for a moment, deciding if he likes it or not. Some babies will take to it like a pig to mud and shoot you dirty looks as if to say *Where have you been hiding this stuff, lady?*

Others aren't interested yet, which you'll know because babies worldwide react the same to things they don't want put in their mouths. The International Brotherhood of Babies Union guidebook gives two clear options: clamp the mouth shut or spit it back at Mommy. Add steely glare for effect.

My friend Trish has a daughter, Maggie, whom we all referred to as the Zen Baby. She would sit on the floor in lotus position, smiling serenely, while all other babies her age were busy crying or whining or trashing the living room. She was completely unflappable. And there were no problems introducing her to food. Until the bananas, that is.

One day I told Trish how my daughter was eating pureed banana by the jarful, so she bought some for Maggie. "She screamed and spat them back at me," Trish told me later. "And I mean she screamed. I've never heard her scream before." Three years later, Trish is still afraid to show her kid a banana.

A few months down the road, feeding gets more complicated, mostly because your baby is more complicated. Baby's got some teeth and is agitating for heartier fare. Now every "dangerous food" warning you've read in all the baby books will come home to roost. You'll spend twenty minutes each morning cutting grapes into quarter sections. You'll peel and slice apples so thin they more resemble french fries than fruit. You'll steam veggies so soft you can't even spoon them intact out of the pot. Then you'll put the whole mess in front of baby and try to act nonchalant as you wait for the choking to begin.

Not to put additional pressure on you, but all the experts say that many of a kid's future eating problems begin now, mostly because you, the parent, try to wrest control over the dinner table. This juncture represents the first and most obvious way a baby can exercise his own free will, and after months of being completely at your mercy, he's got a mind to do it, too. You, however, don't help things by hovering over him until he finishes the parentally sanctioned amount, swallowing your tongue every time he gives a little cough (which he'll do often, if he sees it gets a reaction out of you). It's best for everyone involved if nobody gets high-strung about food.

Easier said than done. Feeding your offspring is a very deep instinct, and when the little nipper won't eat, your first impulse is to FORCE HIM! The baby of course has no interest in doing your pedestrian bidding, and so he refuses to be forced, starting the first of many, many battles of will you will be losing for years to come. You'll pry, you'll prod, you'll beg, bribe, and cajole, all to little effect. And months of watching a parent stoop to any level for the sake of getting him to swallow a spoonful of mush is bound to have some kind of adverse effect on a baby's view of eating. Lots of parents, unnerved by this whole unforeseen conflict, grow to dread feeding time, and pretty soon the whole family looks at mealtime as a chore rather than a pleasure.

♡ ♡ ♡ ♡ ♡ ♡ ♡ ♡ ♡ ♡ ♡ ♡ ♡ ♡ ♡ ♡ ♡ ♡

TOOTH, FORSOOTH!

Babies get their first teeth from about four or five months onward. It's another accomplishment competitive parents like to brag about, even though it's almost entirely up to genetics, and last I checked Harvard wasn't including number of infant teeth by six months as a prerequisite for admission.

Still, it's the rare parent who doesn't feel a secret thrill when he or she sees that little bud of white protruding out of baby's tender gum. Teething means several things for a parent. Among them:

☼ Copious amounts of drool will join the spit-up and breast milk and formula stains all over your T-shirts.

☼ Suddenly, the little sucker can bite.

☼ The fussing and whining and crying you thought had finally calmed down after three months begins anew.

Your baby will be getting a new tooth every couple of minutes for the next two years. The only upshot of this is that it's possible to blame every mystery illness, every crabby mood, and most wet shirts on teething.

♡ ♡ ♡ ♡ ♡ ♡ ♡ ♡ ♡ ♡ ♡ ♡ ♡ ♡ ♡ ♡ ♡ ♡

It doesn't have to be this way at all, of course. If baby turns his nose up at his pablum, shrug it off and try it again later. Babies will eat if they're hungry, and if they feel they're not being given the hard sell. Unfortunately, acting like you don't give a damn whether he eats or not is one of the harder charades of parenting. But it's best to try and perfect it now, in preparation for toddlerhood next year. With any luck you'll have the act down tight by the teenage years.

Hopefully, one of the few foods he actually deigns to eat will be something that falls into one of the five basic food groups as understood on Planet Parenthood. These are:

☀ NUTRITIOUS. Even vaguely nutritious will do. Hey, Cheerios are oats, aren't they? Cheddar cheese Goldfish crackers are . . . well, cheese and . . . fish.

☀ EASY-TO-MAKE. So you won't ever have to utter the words, "But I spent an hour making this for you . . ."

☀ AFFORDABLE IN BULK. So you can shrug when today he eats two bites of whatever he ate a bowl of last night.

☀ NONSTAINING. She may love boysenberries, but have you seen what they do to a couch?

☀ LONG-LASTING IN THE FRIDGE. Sanity, thy name is leftovers . . .

In almost every case, your search for this perfect yet elusive food leads you back to one particular section of the grocery store: Frozen Foods.

Didn't you ever wonder how frozen-food producers stayed in business? Think back to the days when you first moved out of your own parents' house. Remember the thrill of being able to spurn all that cheap, unpalatable processed food you grew up with and buy your own style of groceries? You could choose real butter and freshly baked bread. If you were really upscale, you would buy fresh vegetables at an outdoor farmers' market! No more frozen Tater Tots or lima beans for you! No more American cheese and Wonder Bread sandwiches. You'd never eat another chicken pot pie as long as you lived.

Family dining, like history, I'm afraid, is doomed to repeat itself. By the time your baby is sitting in his high chair eating solid foods, you're spending up to half of your grocery dollar on frozen food items. In the next year, your cupboards and fridge will start to resemble the most stereotypical Saturday morning commercial: macaroni and cheese in the box, frozen peas, frozen corn, Popsicles, Goldfish crackers, bags of apples, gallons of milk, Hostess products.

You don't think so? New parents like to think that they're in complete control of their child's diet, and for the first few years, they are. Once the kid's in kindergarten, however, your best efforts at keeping him sugarfree and all organic will be for naught. He is sure to come home at some point and announce that he traded his cheese sticks and a blue Power Ranger for two Ding Dongs, and Mommy, can't we buy some? Please? Please? Please? C'mawn!

But I digress. We're still in Year One. As much as your pantry is bound to change when you start feeding your baby solid food, all of your evening habits will have to change as well. You're no longer able to do the adult thing after work and sate your hunger with something less than nutritious. No more bowls of cereal. No more bagels. No more tortilla chips and salsa meals. Now you've got someone else to feed, and you absolutely cannot fudge on it. Many times you'll come home from work (or your mate will come home from work, signifying the contractual end of your day, in theory at least), and you'll both be so exhausted the very idea of cooking anything makes you want to cry. Ordinarily you'd order takeout, or make a sandwich, or have a couple of beers and forget about it altogether. But now that's not possible. One of you will haul your tired carcass into the kitchen and begin boiling water and heating the oven for two spoonfuls of frozen peas and one fish stick. You'll calculate how much protein your child has eaten in the last two days and then decide to nix the fish stick in favor of peas and plain pasta noodles. In time you'll start making enough peas and fish sticks for everyone just to save time and brain cells. Strangely enough, it won't help you lose that pregnancy weight that's still hanging around the hips any faster.

COMPETITIVE PARENTING

Tammy and Gordon were sitting in their favorite neighborhood park in San Francisco, airing out three-month-old Jackson. They were enjoying the antics of the toddlers and preschoolers around them when one handsome young boy stopped close by. Tammy smiled at his mother. "What an adorable boy," she said. "How old is he?"

The mother beamed. "He's twenty-two months," she said. "And in the 95th percentile for height and weight."

She went on to add that her son also had a vocabulary of some 456 words.

Gordon almost apologized that his three-month-old hadn't really uttered a sound yet. It was their first experience with the very competitive world of competitive parenting.

Bragging about your kid is as inborn in humans as trying to cheat on your taxes. But these days some people take it to spectacular heights. Indeed, in this competitive era certain kinds of parents can't wait to start their child's brilliant ascent to the top, wherever that may be. They spend their pregnancies staying well within the recommended guidelines for weight gain, play Mozart on headphones pressed to their tummies, and give birth to well-formed babies who score perfect 10s on the Apgar test. They bring these little bundles home to professionally designed nurseries with hand-stenciled walls and Baby-Stim black and white mobiles. Before the child is a year old he's on the waiting list for the "right" preschool program that will get him into the "right" elementary school, then on to the "right" high school, which of course leads right into the hallowed ivy-covered halls of Harvard.

Competitive parenting is easy to laugh about if you have the right attitude. Unfortunately, you yourself will fall prey to the temptation to one degree or another. Even if you vowed you would never be such a parent, you really can't help but admit—and you feel you're being completely objective about this—that your baby is the cutest/smartest/curliest-haired/most imaginative little tyke you've ever met.

My husband and I bragged for months about how pink and unsquishy our daughter was compared to other newborns. We showed her photo to absolute strangers. We gasped at how ugly other new babies were, and had very sincere discussions that should a representative of Baby Gap ever knock on our door we would have to set aside our values and allow her to become the next supermodel.

Then, as time went on, the red squishy babies turned into cute little curly-headed putti, and Annie remained a bald dumpling. She was so mellow it never occurred to her to be an early anything. Not even her hair came in early. She made all the crucial deadlines, thank God, but she wasn't in any rush. She got her first tooth at about three or four months. She rolled from back to front and back again for the first time right on her six-month birthday. She took a step at about thirteen months and then didn't bother with it again until a month later. Talking? At two and a half she makes her desires known, but let's just say she's not as loquacious as she could be. During all of this her father and I, arguably two of the least competitive people in the country (why do you think we live in a one-bedroom apartment?), trip over each other to prove we're not comparing her to anybody else's baby. No sir, not us. We weren't comparing her to her friend Hazel, a five-year-old in a two-year-old's body. Nor to another Anna, who could practically drive a car. Even we had fallen prey. Comparison parenting isn't really something you can avoid. Certain kinds of parents make it an art form, however.

Competitive parenting starts for some people at conception. But it manifests itself in public for the first time usually in the form of labor stories. There's nothing brand-new parents like discussing more than this gory topic. It helps them bond. But inevitably there's one woman in the group who will sit and listen to everyone's horror stories and then beam, "I had a drug-free birth." All the other women will stop midsentence to glower at this woman, whose very tone infers that she alone is the natural Earth Mother, and the rest of them had to rely on modern drugs and machinery to get through the ordeal alive. Even if she doesn't cop the smugger-than-thou tone, others sink into insecurity, which then mutates into bitchiness.

Competitive parents don't wait to get their newborns home to start the festivities. They demand to know the Apgar score their baby received from the doctor. The Apgar test is a misnomer because it's really just a gauge doctors use to evaluate the state of your baby at birth.

Lusty cry or no sound at all? Pink color or the less-good blue color? Reflexes working or not? But some parents cite them like SAT scores: *This is little Miles, two weeks old. He scored very well on the Apgar.* From there on out it's a race to see whose baby holds its head up first, whose baby delivers the first legitimate smile, whose baby sleeps through the night before the three-month mark.

In general, any parent who tells you his or her child is sleeping through the night—the adult definition of night, from, say, 7 P.M. to 6 A.M.—before three months is lying.

The urge to compete with other parents doesn't stop there. There are contests on how big a nursery you have, which pediatrician you procured, how long you breast feed, how much time you take off work, how quickly you lose your pregnancy weight, and of course, where on the percentile chart your baby is compared to his peers.

Chart? Nobody told me about any chart. For the longest time I didn't even know what people were referring to when they invoked the percentile chart. Maybe I wasn't paying attention, or maybe I took the naive view that whatever my doctor was scribbling on at all those well-baby visits wasn't anything I needed to see. Apparently I'm in the minority.

The percentile chart in question is the one that all pediatricians clip to your baby's file that charts how they're growing and gaining weight regularly and within a normal scale. That's all. Apart from serious problems like "failure to thrive" (which most people reading this book, or indeed any parenting book, aren't likely to have to worry about), its importance is strictly clinical. But then doctors will tell you that normal babies will do everything they're supposed to in their own damn time, and whether they walk at eight months or fifteen months doesn't have an ounce of bearing on their potential for making the Olympic soccer team when they're nineteen.

And besides, now my daughter is in the 95th percentile for height for her age, so *nyaaa*.

In an ideal world, we could all live in peace and harmony, there would be no hunger, no unwanted children, no war, and we could all accept each other as we are. Unfortunately, we don't live in that world, we live in this one. As such, we compare our babies and children with other babies and children, and we don't stop until . . . well, as a parent you never stop comparing, not even among your own children—presuming you have any more after this, I mean.

There's an old joke about a Jewish mother whose son was the president of the United States. One day he called her up and invited her to Passover dinner at the White House. "Maybe," she said. "How will I get there?"

"Mother, a limousine will come and pick you up at the door. Air Force One will fly you directly to Washington, and my personal helicopter will deliver you from the airport to the White House lawn."

"Hmph. And who else will be there?"

"Heads of state, international ambassadors, leading intellectuals, and artists from around the world."

"OK, I guess I'll come."

Later that day the mother went to have her hair done. "You know, I'll be spending Passover at my son's house," she told her friend.

"Oooh! The doctor?"

"No. The other one."

MOMMY AND ME

Your reasons for enrolling your baby in a class will vary with your bent and tolerance for life in a messy house alone with a preverbal. You may want to get your child off on the right track for Princeton. You may just want somewhere to drop him off for a few hours a day so you can rejuvenate needed brain cells. Whatever you decide to do, you then have to decide where to do it, and in which class to enroll your little budding Mozart.

Moms and their kids have always congregated for the common good. But it wasn't until the late '70s that actual commercial classes began to proliferate. As America in the '80s got more obsessed with competition, money, and status, the number and breadth of these classes, not to mention their tuition fees, exploded. Today there are thousands of classes a new mom can sign herself up for, beginning with prepartum classes on up through Ivy League summer scholastic camps.

The marketers of these baby classes feed off middle-class American parents' fears that their child won't be able to keep up with the Jones's kid unless he gets the right stimulation from the very start. There's an idea that unless your baby gets out there, gets socialized, starts hearing a second language, drills his ABC flashcards, and begins learning music skills, he'll be an underachiever the rest of his natural days.

Let's look at music. Babies dig it. But these days it's not considered enough to just pop in a CD or turn on the radio (carefully avoiding the *Howard Stern Show*, unless you want your child's first words to be "I am Fartman"). You feel that if you are to be considered a Good Parent, you must enroll your child in a music class by the time he can grasp a maraca. Music classes for the preverbal set are now a healthy industry, and there are dozens of national players, with tortured names like Kindermusik and Music Together. The days of impromptu baby jam sessions in Aunt Bertha's basement are long gone. Today, these classes distribute professional, glossy songbooks and trademark opening songs. Many even have websites. Teachers defect from one to another like free-agent baseball players, and all compete viciously for your baby and his tuition dollars. Reams of new research showing that early music can raise IQ and boost standardized test scores have only fueled the rush to enroll junior. One company boasts that it has children as young as three composing their own songs, which sounds great if you want your kid on the fast-track to Juilliard, but not great if you think the only composing three-year-olds should be doing is of mudpies in the backyard.

All cynicism aside, many gatherings that fall under

the rubric of "classes" actually serve a useful purpose. Lots of them are nothing more than excuses for groups of moms to get out of the house and have coffee with other moms—an extremely worthwhile goal, as you may already have realized. Breast-feeding groups are a good way for a new mom to learn the tricks of that trade and bond with other moms in the lactation boat. It's the classes with tuition fees that start crossing the line.

Let's be clear about one thing, though. Under a year, no child gives a hoot about any other child and will blindly crawl right over another en route to an interesting block. Kids don't play socially, much less politely, until they're about three years old, so there goes the socialization excuse. Moreover, research shows that children don't get a whole lot out of a structured classroom environment until about that age as well, so as far as intellectual stimulation is concerned, unleashing your tot in a park filled with other tots is as good as enrolling him in a $150 kiddie-gym semester. So until then, just admit it: these classes are for you, Mom.

Of course, the other moms might just irritate the hell out of you, in which case you really are showing up to give the baby something to do. That's nothing to be ashamed of. As you quickly learned in your search for new-parent friends, not everyone with a baby is someone you want to hang out with. If the mommies at Mommy and Me are just too Junior League for you to stomach, you can still have a fun time by yourself, alone in the corner with your cup of coffee. Here are some things you can do at a baby class when you can't stand the company:

☼ Stare at the twenty-year-old nannies and make them think you're a parental spy.

☼ Make up creative alternative lyrics for the baby songs they teach in class. *The wheels in my head go rot, rot, rot . . .* (sung to the tune of "The Wheels on the Bus").

☼ Try to start a baby Macarena line.

☼ Announce that someone's SUV is getting towed and watch the room empty.

DAY CARE BLUES

Maybe you're rich. Maybe you're Murphy Brown or you took a company with "dot com" at the end of its name public and never have to think about money again for the rest of your life. Maybe when it came to the question of work and day care, you simply had an agency send over a British nanny to raise junior and got back to your tennis game. If so, please keep it to yourself; none of us wants to hear it.

For the rest of us, the conundrum of work and day care is a major and very ugly shock. It's a stinging reminder that, in America at least, parenting is a nuisance to the free-market economy.

When and if to return to work is a decision that

must be left up to the new mom and dad and should not be made until after the baby is born and all first-month hormones have left the scene. I personally know hard-core career women who had their first child and lost all interest in climbing the corporate ladder and now use their cell phones to remind their husbands to pick up more milk and diaper wipes on the way home. Likewise, I've known women who were planning on staying home who ran screaming from the roost after three short months, women who heave huge sighs of relief after dropping baby off at day care, where he's safe in more competent hands. There is no way to know into which camp you fall, or indeed any of the camps in between, until you've had your baby and had a few months to digest your situation. You may surprise yourselves.

But at some point, and this is no surprise, the decision will have to be made. All too often, the checkbook makes it for you.

Put aside for a moment the modern argument of whether a woman should downsize her career plans when she has children. Let's assume then that there is a sizable population for whom working is not a lifestyle or professional choice but a pay-the-rent-or-live-in-the-shelter choice. After working up to your due-date, spending an expensive twenty-four hours in the hospital, and then enjoying your six-week unpaid leave of absence, you might have no choice but to return to the daily grind in order to make ends meet. Unless you have relatives who can help you out, you're suddenly plunged into the sickening world of finding decent, safe day care that doesn't bankrupt you. How do you do this? Ah yes, how indeed.

The only people you can turn to in this situation are your new-parent friends, and the larger underground community of Parents Anonymous. Working on the theory of concentric circles, you tell all your friends with small children that you are on the lookout for day care, and hope to hell they know other new parents you don't, who in turn might know somebody who can help you. If you can tap into the parental zeitgeist, the truth is out there. You just have to find it.

Finding good day care is like finding an apartment in a city like San Francisco. There's far too much demand and far too little supply. What looks really good you can't remotely afford, and what you can afford makes you want to run screaming back to Des Moines. Finding a happy medium takes one part connections, one part luck, and two parts persistence.

You will have horror stories. Every parent has day care horror stories. They're part of what makes your outer Teflon coating so tough. You'll make a list of possible day care places for your child, and you'll call each and every one. Some you'll discount out of hand when people who don't speak your language answer the phone, or when you hear the screams of many children in the background, or the sound of industrial machinery being operated. Some you will go visit and see fifteen children in various stages of undress watching Barney reruns. Others will appear perfectly acceptable on the surface, but will call you the night before you're due to bring your child in to tell you that the state has suddenly revoked their license.

Eventually, because you have no choice, you'll find a day care place that suits your personal style and needs. And you'll write that big check, the biggest one you'll write each month next to the mortgage or rent check, and agree to bring your baby in next week. And that's when the real fun begins.

You don't know terror until you've handed your firstborn over to a stranger for the first time. In fact, that's just the worst part; the whole first day pretty much sucks. You have to get up at some obscene hour in order to have time to prepare both yourself and baby for delivery by 8:30 A.M. You cry the entire morning (and so does baby), and you drive to the day care center with what can only be described as a block of cement in your stomach. You hand your child over to a woman you've only met once before while your firstborn eyes you with confusion, then betrayal: *Et tu, Mommy?* Then you stumble into the car with her cries ringing in your ears and speed to your miserable job, which grows ever more irrelevant in your estimation with every mile you put between you and your child. The rest of the day is an utter wash. Baby's probably having a grand time, chewing on all the new toys and marveling at the other kids, but you and your mate are sitting at work chewing your fingernails into bleeding stumps and imagining day care horror stories even Hollywood couldn't dream up. Absolutely no work gets done, and come 5 P.M. you're both scratching at the front lobby door with your car keys. You drive like teenage boys across town to pick up your angel, who pretends she doesn't recognize you, and who then screams the entire way home like you just kidnapped her from heaven. You spend the evening checking her body for bruises or strange marks, while giving in to her every demand to assuage your horrible guilt. In twelve short hours you get to do it all again.

Another day care option is the nanny. If you can make enough to pay somebody $10 to $15 an hour to watch your kid, you at least get the benefit of having her come to you. Downsides include paying somebody else a portion of your salary (anywhere from "all" to "more than half of") and not being able to write any of it off unless you can also afford to pay taxes on it. When you're that rich, why are you rushing off to work anyway? Another downside is that sooner or later your child starts calling your nanny Mommy. One story making the rounds in a park I frequent is of a wealthy, Type-A woman (there are lots of them here in San Francisco) who goes through nannies like bedsheets, firing them every six months or when her child starts crying for them at night, whichever comes first.

How about an au pair? Another painfully flawed option that comes in attractive young European packages. Although the idea of having a winsome young woman with a European accent live in your extra room and care for your children is an attractive notion (and it will certainly thrill your husband, no matter what he says), what you're really getting is another kid—a teenager.

A woman I worked with back in my twenties, I'll call her Mel, used to come in every morning with fresh stories of horror about her Dutch au pair, a pretty nineteen-year-old who'd come for the year to live with her family and mind her two small children. "I sat up half the night worrying about Stella," she told me one Monday morning. "She took off for the weekend on Friday night, and when she wasn't home by 8 P.M. Sunday I started to worry we'd find her body in a dumpster." Never mind who was going to watch the kids. Stella eventually made it back—after midnight—hung over and surly. She barely made it up the next morning.

Poor Mel. This was her only day care option, but the problems with Stella were many. Stella was young and Stella was pretty. Stella also came from a small town in Holland and didn't seem to grasp certain cultural differences between here and there. She accepted rides home from men, for example—men who stopped to make wolf noises at her from their cars. She gave her phone number—Mel's phone number—to construction workers. She stayed out late at night and slept in the next morning as Mel tried to get her kids ready for school and herself for work. Stella would get busted trying to buy alcohol. Stella listened to bad Euro-rock. But the kids loved her, so Stella stayed.

By the end of the summer, however, Stella was in full adolescent rebellion. First she got a boyfriend—of the much older variety who hang out in bars. Then she started coming home drunk. Finally—"Well, Stella's crashed our car," Mel told us one August morning. The kids weren't hurt, but Mel and her husband decided there was no further need to live with a teenager before they had to and shipped Stella back from whence she came.

In the end, there is no ideal day care arrangement. You can only hope to find something that works for your particular situation. Until this baby starts school (another conundrum entirely), you will forever battle the child care question. Steel yourselves now.

AS IF STAYING HOME ISN'T WORK

May I just pontificate here on a topic? It's my book, after all.

If ever there was a topic that turned sister against sister and friend against friend, this one is it. This is the fierce debate that's gone on since the '70s, when women began working outside the home in sizable numbers. Now that a whole generation of women has come of age under the idea that we can and should have careers, the argument has gotten even more heated. It's an unwinnable situation, because no matter what you end up doing, you're damned if you do and you're damned if you don't.

If you decide to stay at home with your baby, you're derided as just a housewife, or worse, a rich lady of leisure who can afford not to work. You're told you wasted your education, that you're not being productive and you're losing all marketable job skills you once had. People at parties glaze over when you tell them what you do. Working moms dismiss you.

If you go back to work, you're derided as a selfish career woman who cares more about her personal fulfillment than about her own child. You're asked why you even bothered to have a baby in the first place, since you never see it, and you're blamed for all manner of social ills said to be caused by "latchkey kids." People question your priorities. Stay-at-home moms dismiss you.

Neither of these arguments gets women anywhere. The bigger problem every new family should be banding together to fight is that of our society speaking out of both sides of its mouth. American politicians love to talk about our "family values," but then they come up with nonsolutions like twelve weeks of unpaid family leave, or they table issues like universal health coverage or affordable day care that really affect new families. Maybe when our country puts its money where its mouth is and becomes truly family friendly we'll be able to calm down about this issue. Don't hold your breath, though.

THE VOICE OF IDIOCY

A few of us mom friends settled in the other day to watch home videos of ourselves last year, when our collective progeny were in the six-to-eight-month set. We were amazed at how little they were, how hairless, how helpless compared to the toddler avengers we now had. But the thing that stood out most was the way we comported ourselves with our babies, the way we spoke to them, coddled them, cajoled them into doing every trick in their repertoires.

We were sickening.

"We sound like such . . . mommies!" despaired Meg.

"They're gonna hate us for this when they're teenagers," agreed Mata.

"Do I really have such an irritating voice?" I pondered.

In case you're one of the two new parents on the planet without a video camera, let me affirm for you that to the outside world, you've become a blithering idiot when addressing your child. Squealing, dancing around, asking stupid questions: *Is my Jordan-borden, pudd'n an' pie the cutest boy in the whole wide world? Is he? Izzhhee!? YES HE IS! GIVE DADDY A BIG KISS! A BIIIIIGGGGG KISSY!* Civilians in the room stand horrified, and they begin to move away as you launch into getting your baby to perform. *What sound do cows make, Jordan? Jordan? Come on now, you said it in the car. Jordan? Say moo. Mooo! MOOOO!*

Jordan will never say *moo*. Not when you want him to, anyway. Not in a million years. It's in the Baby Union Guide: No performing in Public and absolutely NO talking on the phone to Grandma.

Of course, your fellow parents understand completely. You can't be blamed for trying. Who can help squeaking at the perfect cuddliness of babyhood? Not for nothing these are called the Kodak Months. Your baby is so indescribably wonderful at home you naturally want her to perform for others. You just have to be able to step back and realize what an ass you're making of yourself. Do not look to your spouse to alert you—he or she is under the same spell. Try, at least, to remember how it was before you had children, when the sight of dancing parents made you cross to the other side of the street.

chapter 5

APPROACHING ONENESS

(8–12 Months)

"Three stages of a parent's life: Nutrition, dentition, tuition."

—MARCELENE COX,
LADIES HOME JOURNAL (1945)

What? A year already? My, how time flies when you're up to your collarbones in Desitin and strained peaches.

The first year of parenthood is like the Year That Never Was. It exists in a unique time/space vortex that never again occurs in nature, not even with the birth of your second child. It's the ultimate in Zen living— utterly and completely in The Now. You spend hours each day marveling at the glow of your baby's skin, and then you spend more hours wiping the drool from that skin and cleaning the poop off that skin and rubbing sunblock into that skin. Your future scheming these days leans more toward getting baby to the midmorning Kindergym class before he falls asleep than taking over the corporate world. Your day-to-day life has been

♡ ♡ ♡ ♡ ♡ ♡ ♡ ♡ ♡ ♡ ♡ ♡ ♡ ♡ ♡ ♡ ♡ ♡

USEFUL TERMS

BABYPROOFING Stripping your home of all valuables, breakables, and heavy objects that your newly mobile baby might be interested in pulling down onto himself.

BARNEY, ELMO, LAA-LAA, AND BLUE A purple dinosaur, a red monster, the larger girl Teletubby (she's yellow), and a blue dog. By the time your child is two you'll have seen every episode of all of these and know all the theme songs by heart.

CARE PROVIDER The baby-sitter. And they don't get no paltry $2 a night anymore, either. A good baby-sitter will cost you upwards of $10 an hour in a lot of cities these days. Day care providers, also essentially baby-sitters, are another story entirely.

MMR The dreaded measles/mumps/rubella shot your baby has to get between one year and fifteen months. Ouch!

SIBS Short for siblings, as in brother and sister, as in, you don't even want to think that far ahead yet . . .

♡ ♡ ♡ ♡ ♡ ♡ ♡ ♡ ♡ ♡ ♡ ♡ ♡ ♡ ♡ ♡ ♡ ♡

completely co-opted by the worry, the care, the feeding, and the entertainment of this third party.

When all is said and done, you can't really recall any details. When newer parents ask you what happens in the fifth month, you can only stare at them blankly. *Fifth month? Uh, let me find my notes . . .* At the time, you knew as much as your pediatrician about the emotional, physical, and mental development of the five-month-old infant, that much you remember. But then came the sixth month, and like clockwork your brain flushed clean of the previous month's mountain of information to make room for the complete encyclopedia on the next.

Fortunately, you know just what to do in practice, even if you can't put all the details down on paper. It's a whole lot like swimming. Once you learn you never forget. You'll be able to go to your friends' house to visit their newborn and pick up that newborn with a skill and confidence that make your friends fall to their knees in awe. *Please stay for dinner,* they'll beg, *and grant us more of your divine wisdom!* You'll chuckle as your pregnant friends talk about their plans for having the baby sleeping through the night by six weeks so everyone can go back to work. You know what cradle cap is and how to get rid of it. You have fail-safe burping techniques not shown in books. You have mastered the mystery of the car seat.

These are the same skills grandmothers have (although theirs are much more highly developed), and when you can demonstrate them with skill and good humor, you know you're a full-fledged dweller on Planet Parenthood.

As any grandma could have told you, the first year with your first baby is the killer. These are the only twelve months of your life that turn you into a parent. No number of babies after that has the same effect, so complete was the mutation after the first one. By the end of Year One, you're a hardened parent. You don't scare easily anymore.

And good thing, too. Because at this point, your baby is starting to seem, well, less like a baby and more like an actual person. She's walking or making ready to walk. She can point to whatever she's interested in. She might be saying a few words. Her likes and dislikes are very clear. Her personality is fully formed, and she's a master at getting you to do her every bidding. From here it's one big slippery slope into toddlerhood, which is a completely different parenting enchilada.

You're going to need all your newfound skills to navigate the next twelve months. Good luck.

LAST ONE WALKING IS A . . .

If ever there was an unspoken goal you'd been working toward for lo these many months, walking is it. Walking is a huge deal in parental circles, replacing everything else on the competitive parent's playlist and even sending normally easygoing parents into fits of anxiety. For the few months baby spends getting the nerve up for a solo launch, everyone involved is obsessed with the task. Grandparents call for the daily update. Coworkers start avoiding you for fear you'll

♡ ♡ ♡ ♡ ♡ ♡ ♡ ♡ ♡ ♡ ♡ ♡ ♡ ♡ ♡

ADVANCED PARENTING

Oh, the skills you possess now that you've been a parent for one whole year. Here are some feats you can now perform with aplomb. Watch your friends with newborns stare at you in awe as you:

☼ diaper and dress a moving tot

☼ deal with a two-alarm poop in under five minutes with only three wipes

☼ leave the house on twenty minutes' notice (as opposed to the two hours you needed in the first week)

☼ interpret all cries, whines, and gurgles and respond accordingly

☼ discuss vaccines, doses, timetables, and efficacy rates

☼ accurately gauge the age of other babies to within two weeks

☼ make macaroni and cheese without reading the box

☼ maintain an outward calm in the face of all tantrums

☼ schlepp

♡ ♡ ♡ ♡ ♡ ♡ ♡ ♡ ♡ ♡ ♡ ♡ ♡ ♡ ♡

spend twenty minutes detailing baby's latest pseudostep accomplishment to them during their break. The camcorder batteries are charged (and you have two more juicing up just in case . . .), and the camera is loaded and nearby. You don't know when it's actually going to happen, but by gum you're going to capture it for posterity when it does.

The baby is more obsessed than all of you. Not only is he heeding nature's call for upward mobility, he's beginning to glean that he could have much more fun and could get to those interesting things on the shelf if he could just . . . stand up and move a little to the . . . right. He's on his own schedule, and no amount of prodding or begging on your part will make him take those first steps before he's ready to do so. He's completely ignoring you on that issue. He has found one new use for you, however—you are his walking prop.

Remember that *Alien* movie (The third? The fourth?) in which the heroine cages herself in a giant, hydropowered robot to do battle with the much stronger alien? This is sort of the way your baby now sees you. You are a useful tool of self-propulsion. Your legs and balance are stronger than his, so he makes use of them to achieve his objective, whether it's getting up and down the hall or going around and around the kitchen divider. Now you are his personal walker, and having you walk him becomes his sole reason for getting up every morning at dawn. It also becomes your biggest reason for finding a good chiropractor.

Just as you're realizing the wisdom of having children at nineteen, when your back would have been more up to the task, baby decides he's ready for a solo performance. When the big day finally arrives, it *will* resemble every commercial ever made that uses a toddling baby to jerk a tear out of you. One day or night your baby will just let go of whatever couch or chair he's propping himself up on, and, leering and lurching like a drunk, he'll take one step, two steps, maybe even three, toward your outstretched arms. You'll be screaming and laughing and clapping your hands, calling your own parents and all your friends, and using up whole rolls of film and videotape. You'll be puffed up with a pride you've never felt before, a wholly parental joy that's got nothing to do with you and everything to do with your baby, who is probably quietly wondering what you two are making such a fuss over.

After you've calmed down, I recommend that you take a good long look at your baby. What you now have is a mobile unit. A thing that is capable of moving away from you without the sense to know why it shouldn't. What you now have is a roaming death wish, and it is your job to monitor it during all waking hours. Once the novelty wears off for you in a few weeks (it doesn't wear off for baby for a few years), you'll start to wonder why you were ever in such a hurry to get him upright.

For the foreseeable future, walking is your baby's reason for being. He loses interest in everything else that used to give him pleasure, including eating, sleeping, and nursing. This is nature's sign that it's time to wean, if you haven't already. No baby on the go wants to stop for lunch, so you may as well keep your shirt buttoned. There is no more lunchtime as you knew it, and you'll gradually take to following the baby around the house all day trying to sneak pieces of apple or cheese into him as he opens his mouth to laugh. Around this time, that much-valued morning nap goes the way of the dodo, and the afternoon nap gets drastically abbreviated. Bedtimes, too, become traumatic, mostly because the baby knows he will have to stop walking, and he doesn't want to stop walking, not for anything, even though by the end of the day he's walking into walls because he's so worn out. Eventually you'll have to do the adult thing and forcibly get him ready for bed, put him down, and let the screams of indignation ring through your house until he passes out in exhaustion. He'll be there in the morning, standing in his crib and pumping his legs, ready to run off like a windup toy the moment you set him down. All you can do is make another pot of coffee and follow him in his travels.

But what if your baby isn't walking yet? Calm down. He will. All babies, unless they're developmentally disabled in some way, will eventually get vertical. But despite what competitive parents would have you believe, whether they walk at eight months or fifteen months is largely a function of genetics. Ask your own mothers when you took your first steps; oftentimes you'll see junior follow a similar flight path. Size and gender don't seem to make a difference at all. I've seen the tiniest of ten-month-old girls running around a baby store, and I've seen hefty fourteen-month-old boychicks who weren't in any particular hurry to toddle.

This kind of huge spread should reassure parents, but instead it has the opposite effect. Since walking is one of the most obvious developmental landmarks, it's not something you can fudge. It's not like talking, where you can boast a vocabulary of 150 words from your child, 149 of which sound like gibberish to everyone else. Either they're walking or they're not. You'll sit stiff-lipped in the park and watch kids younger than yours pull themselves up and waddle over to another bench. When those babies' parents ask whether your child is walking yet, you'll twitch uncomfortably. "Well of course he's walking," you lie. "But only when he feels like it, and never in public."

The truth of the matter is that walking is like the great divide in parenting. There are those parents with babies not yet mobile (which in retrospect seems pretty easy in comparison) and those parents sprinting after babies well on their way toward the stairs, the street, the muddy puddles.

Which brings us to footwear.

How you feel about shoes for baby says a lot about who you are as a person. Are you going to run out to the Stride Rite and plop down $50 for a pair of Timberland boots that your son will grow out of by the end of the month? Or are you the sort who doesn't see anything wrong with the $1.99 pair of used, strangely moist sneakers you found at the thrift store. Perhaps you take a middle ground and go to Mervyn's or Target for their nice selection of $10 to $20 shoes. Are you boycotting anything with Disney characters on it? (If so, you've narrowed your choices by half.) How do you feel about Nike's labor practices in Indonesia? And what about the need for ankle support—fact or fiction?

Nothing makes you feel more grown up than standing in a store trying to decide what kind of shoes to buy your child. Guaranteed your mate will have completely different tastes than you, and you'll have a very public fight over Little Mermaid sneakers vs. black patent Mary Janes. Best to settle such stylistic questions quickly, since you'll be back buying bigger shoes next month. Look at it this way: at least now you have a way to keep Baby's socks on.

WALK ON THE OUTSIDE

Great. So your kid's walking now. Did you ever think about how he's gonna react when you take him outside?

No, I can see that you didn't.

Babies love the outside world. Walking babies, so much more. There's so much to see and do and taste. Look at the cars! They go so fast! Look at the grass and the dog poop and the puddles! Hey, let's make for the driveway!

Bringing your newly mobile child outside for her first walk ranks right up there with first doctor appoint-

♡ ♡ ♡ ♡ ♡ ♡ ♡ ♡ ♡ ♡ ♡ ♡ ♡ ♡ ♡ ♡

WHAT YOU'LL NEED

(8-12 Months)

☼ **A GOOD CHIROPRACTOR.** Or a good yoga class to soothe your aching back.

☼ **NERVES OF STEEL.** For all your outdoor adventures with the toddler avenger.

☼ **PAPER TOWELS.** In 24-pack cases. Do you have to ask?

☼ **A GOOD PARK.** To let off toddler steam.

☼ Ok, Ok. Maybe a **MINIVAN** would be nice right about now.

♡ ♡ ♡ ♡ ♡ ♡ ♡ ♡ ♡ ♡ ♡ ♡ ♡ ♡ ♡ ♡

ment and first time left at day care on the parental Fret-O-Meter. There are too many variables out there, and your baby has too little sense. She's a walking question mark and wants to explore everything from the pigeon poop to the car muffler. Then she wants to taste it. You, the parent, are now called upon to be way more vigilant than you think you can possibly be, and going outside is no longer much fun. Not when baby's on the ground, I mean. And at this age, being strapped into a stroller or backpack is not where the baby wants to be.

But you have to go out sometimes. Monitoring the newly mobile baby while in the great outdoors is a full-time gig. When there are two of you it's possible to get things done—as long as one of you shadows the child full-time. Venturing outside solo is more challenging. It requires nerves of steel and the paranoia of a Secret Service agent. Get some dark glasses and a suit and you can even look like a Secret Service agent.

Flanking a new walker on the outside is also an exercise in focus and concentration. You must learn to close out all competing stimuli and keep your eye on the prize. Take your eye off the tot for even a moment . . . and she's gone! For several seconds you'll experience the kind of stomach-dropping terror only people in crashing airplanes must feel. Your mind races through several layers of horror as you swing yourself around and start calling her name, and when you finally spy her, racing toward the apples, you'll hurl yourself through space to nab her. She's giggling up a storm, you're sweating, other people are staring. Those toddler leashes you used to disparage really begin to make sense right about now.

NO

Up until now, you, the all-knowing, all-seeing Parent, dictated the course of baby's life. You decided what she'd wear and what she'd eat. You picked a nice, sunny corner of the living room and laid baby there on a baby blanket of your choosing. You decided on the park du jour. Your days of playing the benevolent despot, however, are numbered.

By the one-year mark, your baby is starting to show alarming signs of self-actualization. These signs are very cute at first, until the first time you're foiled in your parental duties by the will of the child herself. Maybe the first indication of things to come was the mouth clamped resolutely shut at an offering of lunch, making it known to you in no uncertain terms that after today, there would be no more steamed peas, thank you. Perhaps there was the balking at getting into the stroller, or a reluctance to enter the bathing chamber. These changes will happen quite suddenly and without warning. One day your baby will be the compliant creature she always was, and the next she will fight you tooth and claw over everything, reacting to the common diaper change in a way that suggests, to the passerby, anyway, the use of extreme violence and cruelty on your part. You won't know what to make of this at first. Is she sick, you'll wonder? Is she teething? Then you'll notice that glint in her eye, the set of her jaw . . . that furrow in her brow . . .

The time of *No* has arrived.

No is the most powerful tool your baby now has at his disposal. *No* is easy to say. It's definitive. And without fail it gets a big reaction out of you two. If you're a one-year-old, this is total entertainment.

Let's put your coat on and go to the park, shall we?

No.

Let's get back in the stroller and go home now.

No.

It's dinnertime! Are we hungry?

No.

Bath?

No.

Bed?

No. NO!! NNNOOOOOOO!!!!!!

The *No* time often coincides with the walking time and the time nature has decreed for little brains to mature enough to feel some sense of individuality. For the first time in their lives, the little tykes have figured out

♡ ♡ ♡ ♡ ♡ ♡ ♡ ♡ ♡ ♡ ♡ ♡ ♡ ♡ ♡ ♡ ♡ ♡ ♡

TO PARTY OR NOT TO PARTY?

Maybe you're breathing a sigh of relief on hitting the one-year mark as a parent. Or maybe you've got enough energy to celebrate. If this is the case, think long and hard about what kind of celebration you want to share with the world. I know, I know—it's hard to contain your enthusiasm here, and everyone loves a good party, right? For your information, one-year birthday parties fall into three basic categories:

THE EMBARRASSING BASH. Drop $5k on hiring clowns, ponies, etc. Invite everyone from your play group, neighborhood, and Gymboree class. Sit and watch babies as they become overwhelmed and either pitch into tantrums or glaze over and drool on their party

♡ ♡ ♡ ♡ ♡ ♡ ♡ ♡ ♡ ♡ ♡ ♡ ♡ ♡ ♡ ♡ ♡ ♡ ♡

that they are separate entities from their parents and as such should have their say in matters.

Unfortunately, this is only the beginning of an ugly trend. Your baby's growing inclination toward negativity will get worse—much, *much* worse—before it gets better. It peaks for different babies at different times, depending on inborn temperament, but in general this is where the term "terrible twos" originates. Tantrums, holding of breath, throwing food, screaming. The first utterance of the word *no* portends all of these.

♡ ♡ ♡ ♡ ♡ ♡ ♡ ♡ ♡ ♡ ♡ ♡ ♡ ♡ ♡ ♡ ♡

clothes. Try and fail to engage them in a rousing rendition of "Happy Birthday." Calm them when they panic at the sight of the ponies and clowns. Open their many presents for them and don't bother wondering why they seem more interested in the boxes they came in.

THE NOD. Spend $15 and make cupcakes for you, baby, and maybe one baby friend and her parents. Let babies smash cupcakes into their hair and go play with their one, unwrapped present. Take a photo to send to the grandmas.

WHAT BIRTHDAY? Spend nothing and watch baby spend the day blissfully unaware that she's hit a milestone. Spend the money Grandma and Grandpa send to hire a baby-sitter and go out to dinner as a reward for making it this far.

♡ ♡ ♡ ♡ ♡ ♡ ♡ ♡ ♡ ♡ ♡ ♡ ♡ ♡ ♡ ♡ ♡

This stage terrifies a lot of parents. Though by now you're feeling pretty confident about routine baby care, the concept of discipline throws you. What do you say to a one-year-old who insists on throwing wooden beads at the cat? How do you handle public tantrums? This is when the real parenting comes in, when you are called upon as an alleged grown-up to do the right thing and steer your child away from his innate evil impulses. Without fail, this leaves you feeling incompetent and weak, forcing you to resort to the very cliches you swore you'd never use on your children: *Don't make Mommy say it again*, and *Daddy's going to be very upset when he gets home*. You have to start being firm about bedtimes, and about things like how many spoonfuls of soup are acceptable before dinnertime is over. Hey, nobody likes being the heavy, but somebody has to start teaching your child right from wrong. And since you're the alleged grown-up now, it looks like the somebody has to be you.

Bet you're starting to understand how sheepish Dad must have felt when he grounded you after that six-pack incident.

MORE IDEALS OUT THE DOOR

You were such an idealistic young parent. You were going to breast feed exclusively through the first year. You were going to use all-cotton diapers and clad him only in natural organic fibers. You were going to carry him all day long in a baby sling and sing folk songs to him as he slumbered at night.

That didn't last three months, if you're like most people. You very quickly learned what tools or methods kept the baby from screaming, and you implemented them without looking back. Pacifier? Fine. Apple juice throughout the day? Whatever. Disposable diapers? Of course. If you haven't dropped at least one of your high-minded ideals by this point you're obviously dangerously controlling and obsessive, and you may not have many friends anymore.

The fact is, by this juncture you have realized the golden rule of parenthood: compromise. If you can whittle down an ideal to the point that it is palatable for baby, everyone can sleep easier (or longer, anyway). Even at this tender age, most babies have fully grasped the notion that getting half of everything they want is better than nothing at all. In this respect, they're ready to work with you.

For example: You believe your one-year-old should still nap twice a day, as she did in the early months. Your one-year-old, however, doesn't concur. You compromise by putting her in her crib with a good book and letting her have a quiet time for half an hour so both you and she can have a breather. You don't insist she fall asleep. If you're lucky, she won't insist on getting up. You reunite in half an hour, both happier people.

Or the TV dilemma: You were absolutely against the idea of videos when your child was born. No passive reception for him, no-siree. You yourself spent much of your childhood sitting slack-jawed in front of the idiot box, watching "Scooby Doo," "Speed Racer," and endless "Brady Bunch" reruns, and you had no intention of letting your own progeny suffer the same damage. You were going to stimulate his little brain yourself, with homemade flash cards and black and white tactile learning toys. Twelve months later, you admit that you vastly underestimated the power of a good "Sesame Street" alphabet video on your peace of mind. A whole thirty minutes of silence and calm for $10? Cheap at twice the price! By the time he's three you will have amassed a great kiddie video collection, each title a fierce protector of your mental well-being. Now you can be heard telling new mothers that the Teletubbies are totally undeserving of all the bad press they get.

Ideals are as varied as parents. But in general any aspect of baby care that is maligned by modern-day middle-class American parents qualifies as an ideal that can be more or less embraced without harmful consequences. Talk to your own parents for pointers on how they did things when you were an infant.

STUFF YOUR KID ISN'T DOING YET

Woe betide the modern parent. Back in the days before a baby's development was studied, analyzed, dissected, deconstructed, charted, graphed, and made

into multimedia events, parents were blissfully unaware that little Johnny didn't have quite the motor
skill set for his age-group. He caught up whenever he
caught up, and nobody was the wiser. Today, every new
parent is made hypervigilant when it comes to whatever milestone the books say his or her progeny should
be attaining. The literature says Junior should have
four or more teeth by his fifth month and he only has
three? You can spend whole afternoons wringing your
hands in front of the pediatric dentist, who won't be
able to do anything anyway, and Junior will have those
errant teeth long before you pay off the dentist bills.
My suggestion to you is that you ignore the literature
and wait. There's a huge swatch of time on either end
of a milestone into which "normal" can still fall. Yeah,
it will kill you to hear the neighbor's kid arguing
rhetorically with his parents (and winning) when your
kid, same age, is still pointing wildly and muttering,
"Dat? Dat?" But steel yourself anyway. He's (probably)
normal.

That said, there are a few milestones worth fretting
about more than others, not that fretting about them
will make any difference. These are usually practical
matters that affect your quality of life, and as such, the
baby isn't interested in acquiescing at all.

Sleeping through the night, for example. Now what
in tarnation happened here? All the books say a baby
should be sleeping soundly through the night by three
months, and here it is, pushing a year, and a solid eight
hours of sleep is still just a memory. This is more com-

mon than anyone would have you believe. It's the dirty little secret of parenting: nobody likes to advertise the fact that they're still getting up in the middle of the night to minister to their child because it invites disparaging comments, even visits from the Parent Police. Even though it's you who has to live with sleep deprivation, the general public will feel no compunction telling you what you're doing wrong. You're still breast feeding, and the child must be hungry, they'll conclude, and that's what you get for trying to breast feed this long. Or: You're coddling her. You're responding to his every whine. You're making him too dependent on you, and so on, and so on. Only you and the baby know what is really going on here. Or maybe only the baby knows. At any rate, it takes too much energy to explain why you're not getting a full night's sleep this far into the year, so take your cue from baby and don't offer an explanation to anyone.

The cup thing is another stumper. All the books say that a baby should be able to drink from a cup by one year. From a physiological standpoint, this may well be true. But again, baby's got his own ideas. In the ideal world, Good Parents effortlessly wean baby off the breast or bottle onto the cup. In the ideal world, baby nods agreeably and happily takes to a strange contraption that has neither the comfort nor the warmth of a bottle or breast. More typically, however, babies have no interest in these strange cup usurpers. They refuse to hold one, or if they do, they hold it only for as long as it takes to inspect the contents and pour it into their laps. For flair maybe they'll hurl it across the room. You might well stay home from any first-birthday parties you're invited to because of your child's unpredictability with drinking vessels. And giving up the bottle by a year? I don't think so. You can forget about that myth for another year or so. Baby plans to suck it up, so you may as well too.

And what about Mamma and Dadda, huh? Wasn't your progeny supposed to have recognized the two of you by now? She might be coming along very nicely with other nouns: ball, pup, cup. So why not the easiest two syllables in the universe? The most important syllables in the universe! Really, you're starting to get insulted. My daughter said Da-da at four months but didn't address me personally until she was almost a year and a half, no matter how hard I drilled her. Sometimes she still calls me Daddy.

No hair is a big deal, too, even though it's the one area where you as parent are held completely blameless. After twelve months, you'd like a little hair to play with, just a little curl to twist in your fingers, or a few strands to tape a bow into. It doesn't seem fair that some babies are born with luxurious manes while your angel goes without. Older, more experienced parents will tell you that prolonged baldness means nothing, that your child could have thick curls by two or stunning flaxen locks at three. But that doesn't do you any good now. You want people to stop mistaking your girl child, the one you dress in pink dresses and purple butterfly hats, for a boy. And you want them to stop referring to your boy as Mr. Clean. Most of all you want to use some of that baby shampoo that's been taking up space in your bathroom for the last year.

SHOPPING EN FAMILLE

By now you've adapted with gusto to your new circumstances. You've observed how your shopping habits have changed and nearly choked over your weekly gro-

♡ ♡ ♡ ♡ ♡ ♡ ♡ ♡ ♡ ♡ ♡ ♡ ♡ ♡ ♡ ♡

WHAT YOU CAN'T DO NOW THAT YOU'RE THE PARENT OF A ONE-YEAR-OLD

Now that you've had some time to gain perspective, you can see that certain aspects of this parenting thing were easier back in the early days, when baby mostly slept, and his needs were few. It was possible to take him out in his baby carrier past his bedtime. You could enjoy a nice meal at a restaurant with him sleeping soundly in the next seat. But now that he's mobile, now that he can voice an opinion and objects loudly to confinement of any sort, those days are gone. Now you have to bow to his schedule, his needs, and his kind of fun. Sorry. This is your life for another two years. Here are a few of the activities you can

♡ ♡ ♡ ♡ ♡ ♡ ♡ ♡ ♡ ♡ ♡ ♡ ♡ ♡ ♡ ♡

♡ ♡ ♡ ♡ ♡ ♡ ♡ ♡ ♡ ♡ ♡ ♡ ♡ ♡ ♡

no longer do when you find yourself the parent of a one-year-old:

☼ EAT OUT AT RESTAURANTS. Unless specifically designated as "Family-Style Dining" (read: bad food, lots of noise), you will not be going out to eat with baby for at least another two years, and by then you've been conditioned to prefer Chuck E. Cheese to Bella Trattoria anyway.

☼ MOVIES. No. Disney movies? No. VCRs were invented with you in mind. Use one.

☼ CAMPING. You're welcome to try, but after you pack all the baby stuff you'll need in the bush, you'll either have to hire a Sherpa or stay home and camp in the backyard.

☼ FOREIGN TRAVEL. You're even <u>thinking</u> about boarding a plane with a one-year-old?

☼ AUSTIN POWERS "SHAG-A-DELIC" DANCE PARTY. Sorry. You're a parent now. You don't get to do these sorts of things anymore. Your baby-sitter does, though.

♡ ♡ ♡ ♡ ♡ ♡ ♡ ♡ ♡ ♡ ♡ ♡ ♡ ♡ ♡

cery bill, which now includes innumerable jars of baby food, gallons of milk, cans of formula, diapers, baby wash, apple juice, and macaroni and cheese by the ton. You've also observed the survival skills of other families, and now you're prepared to follow suit. Heck, you're not proud.

Pile on into that minivan this Saturday and go for a bulk shopping trip to Target. Or Wal-Mart. Or whatever mom-and-pop-killing chain discount store that exists in your part of the country. There's not a lot of reason to venture into one of these places prechild unless you need to buy a minor appliance or some cheap shoes. Now, it's a different story. Not only do you need several minor appliances and a pair of cheap tennis shoes, but lots more for the home and baby as well. The upscale baby stores are fine for a while, before you realize that white lace clothing and $25 baby cups are somewhat impractical. Yes, I know you feel sheepish; I did as well on my first trip into one of these "family emporiums." But take my word for it, you'll be so dazzled once inside that your shame will dissolve before you're even into the kiddie clothes section. From your new, domestically minded point of view, these discount superstores are shopping nirvana.

Picture this: Jumbo packs of disposable diapers—seventy-five for under $15! Baby wipes by the case. Formula by the drum. Ten different kinds of baby bath. Barney slippers and Elmo socks. Baby shoes with Velcro! T-shirts, five for $3! Cheerios in bulk! Goldfish crackers in gallon cartons!!!

Not the kind of shopping spree you used to get excited about, to be sure. But things have changed, haven't they? You don't really have a burning need for cute little red pumps anymore, do you? Or silk suits on sale or new sports equipment. What you need are practical items, and you want them cheap and in bulk. It's guaranteed that you'll be bragging about your finds to your new-parent friends within minutes of getting home and putting Junior down for his nap. You'll be feeling mighty pleased with yourself now that you have two months' worth of diaper backups stored in the garage, or six two-gallon jugs of apple juice in the cellar in case you run out one hot summer day.

Chain discount stores aren't the only places you frequent as a new parent. Toy stores are foreign territories you will soon come to know like a native as well.

Like chain discount stores, there's not a whole lot of reason to venture into a toy store, much less a toy "emporium," after the age of twelve. Soon after the birth of your baby, however, you found that there are a lot of things you can't buy outside of a toy store, such as bath seats and stroller nets and clown night-lights. You entered warily at first, but as you became more knowing as a parent, you learned to understand the lay of the land. Car seats, you learned, could be had more cheaply at the discount chain stores. Bookstores had a wider selection of books. But for everything else from dolls to balls to *Star Wars* action figures, the toy store was the only place to go.

Toy stores still have all the stuff you had as a kid. All the Fisher-Price stuff is there, that popcorn pusher and that animal farm. They still make Slinkies and Barbies and Big Wheels. There's a heck of a lot more TV character stuff than you remember, but that's just a sign of the times. Toy stores also have a huge amount of stuff you didn't have as a kid. They've got gizmos for the sandbox and bath that you're tempted to buy for yourself. They've got acres of plastic push cars and houses and jungle gyms that nobody but the rich kids had back in your day. Now that your baby is approaching his first birthday, the kinds of toys you want for him become more sophisticated. You want push-pull gizmos, and musical instruments that you will hate yourself for buying soon enough. You want the latest Teletubbies video and a Blue's Clues coloring book. You want Legos—the 380-piece set! Toy stores, you'll soon come to realize, are as much about fantasy fulfillment for you as they are for the kids.

Don't get too cozy in these places, though. Toy stores become increasingly dangerous territory as your baby becomes a toddler. By the time your child is three they are to be avoided at all costs if you want to escape with your sanity (and this month's rent money) intact.

THE BIG SETTLE DOWN

The best-laid plans are scrapped when you have your first baby, but by the year mark you're starting to reclaim those plans, and in earnest. After getting your bearings, it's not unusual for the whole family picture to fall into place within months. I know one couple who finished grad school, got the Big Job, had the second baby, bought the first house, found the requisite dog, and upgraded to minivan all within the space of a semester. "I woke up this morning, and I'm my father!"

screamed my friend. Sure, we were laughing, but we both knew he was in an enviable position.

Now that you've acclimated to the idea of yourselves as a family, the instinct to settle down hits hard. No matter what your circumstances, you're looking to upgrade, to find a real job, to find a neighborhood to stay in. Is there a house in your future? A co-op? A bigger apartment? How about a washer/dryer of your very own? A backyard? A place for a swing set? You shudder at the delicious, illicit fantasy of it all.

Some trend guru in the '80s allegedly coined the term "nesting," which means the process of keeping close to home, fluffing your pillows, and filling your home with stuff carted back from the Bed, Bath & Beyond superstore. When you add your first child to the mix, that nesting instinct amplifies threefold, which is why the idea of shopping at family superstores gains great appeal after you've become a parent.

The urge to settle down isn't limited to the notion of nesting, however. Settling down also means putting aside your dreams of action and adventure for the time being. Were you still dreaming of quitting your job and joining the Peace Corps? I have some bad news for you: it's not gonna happen anytime soon. Of course you always read about the couple who do sell everything and paddle off to the deep Congo, kids in tow. But what you never read about is how pissed off the kids are at having to endure such adventure at an age when all they really want is five years of monotony. There's nothing monotonous about the Congo. Plus if you raise a small child in the Congo, the child becomes a Congolese and learns a patois of Bantu and French, and he'll panic when you show him a parka after you've moved back to Minnesota in four years.

Or are you dreaming of selling everything and buying a boat and taking a 'round-the-world jaunt? Sounds great, but it's just not practical with the kids unless you're supremely self-centered and blind to practical matters, such as how do you babyproof your house when your house is a boat on the open seas? Likewise, the time to climb Mt. Everest was before you had children. You might still be able to do it in twenty years' time—although by then you probably won't have the energy. In the meantime, there are lots of comforting books to read on the topic.

You're a family person now. You go to work in the morning and you come home at night and you give your child his dinner and a bath and then you kiss him good night. It's going to be like this for a few more years now. The Merchant Marines will have to wait.

TIME FOR ONE MORE?

If you're going for the mortgage, two cars, dog, and 2.5 kids scenario you'd better hop to it. The textbook-perfect two-year spacing between children means you have to start trying in earnest to beget the next one right about now. Sure, you have until month fifteen to get knocked up, according to the numbers. But who gets pregnant on the first try anymore unless they're sixteen or just alarmingly fertile? Best to start reacquainting yourselves with lots of goal-oriented sex now to get the ovens prepped.

Sort of seems unfair, doesn't it? You're just starting to feel normal again—you can fit back into your prepregnancy jeans, your stomach almost passes muster, you can guffaw spontaneously without peeing your pants—and now it's time to do the whole tedious pregnancy thing over again. No doubt Dad is gritting his teeth as well. He knows this may be the last time he gets any for years to come. Sigh. What price the perfect family?

You may actually be pregnant now—lots of women do the sibling thing one year apart. There's a school of thought that getting it all over with quickly is better than spreading it out. It's utter chaos for the first five years until they start entertaining themselves, but the upshot is you get them all out of the house for college within two years of each other, and you're done!

Or you might be opting to wait. Waiting a few more years might be an attractive choice as well. Introducing another child into the mix when your first is a compliant, rational four-year-old is a whole different experience from bringing one home when she's two and in full defiance mode. You can actually convince a four-year-old that this is *her* baby—like a big, really serious new toy—and get her to cooperate in its care and feeding most of the time.

"Have four or five. Then you don't have time to worry."

—BARBARA FISCHER, MOTHER OF SEVEN

Indeed, when you look at the facts with an objective eye, spacing your children two years apart is the least palatable option of them all. It means you have to suffer through pregnancy with a toddler who would exhaust you even if you didn't weigh thirty extra pounds and have hormones that put you to sleep every night promptly at six. It means that you bring a vulnerable newborn home to a homicidal psychopath not unlike the spurned, jealous woman in *Fatal Attraction*. (If she can't have you then nobody can!) It means you have to somehow live through not only the first three months of constant crying and no sleep, but also with a child at the very zenith of Terrible Two-dom *at the very same time*. What reasonable set of people would choose to put themselves through this?

Millions of reasonable people, apparently. Not long after their child's first birthday, women start coming up pregnant in droves. Like lemmings, one after the other after the other takes the plunge, until you start to wonder what kind of weird parental peer pressure is at work here. "All of Hoboken is pregnant!" howled my friend Linda, who has a two-year-old, and is stopping there.

Think long and hard before planting number two. If you thought it was hard morphing from couple into a family with the first one, subsequent children kill all semblance of your old selves. By now you've probably carved out a reasonably balanced life between the three of you, in whatever incarnation works best for your circumstances. You can still get out sometimes, just the two of you, and you've come to regard Sundays in the park as a pleasant way to pass the day.

Now add another baby. Suddenly, the schedule you worked all year to set up falls apart like a house of cards. Now one of you has to deal with the new baby while the other distracts the toddler during every waking hour. Who makes dinner? Who cleans up? How does anything get done anymore? Why has your two-year-old reverted to infancy?

What's the rush?

You know what the rush is, even if you can't articulate it. You want another one because . . . well, just because. You both know full well what it's going to do to your lives, but you embrace the idea anyway. These last twelve months have demonstrated to your satisfaction that although raising a kid does nothing for your figure, your bank balance, your furniture, or your career, it beats the alternative hands down. So go ahead and have another. Have a few more. Now that you're living on Planet Parenthood, you know what to expect for the rest of your life, to various degrees. And you know your payback will be subtle, if anything at all. But these days, that's all you need.

PLANET PARENTHOOD— ARE WE THERE YET?

Someone up there liked us. We had found a parking spot big enough for Tory and Jon's new station wagon only two blocks from the main drag of the trendy but perennially parking-free Marina District of San Francisco. Tory and I unstrapped the babies from their car seats while the men unloaded the back. First the strollers. Then two huge diaper bags holding everything from a change of clothing to snacks to baby Tylenol in case the teething started again. After that came the toy buckets and shovels and other gear for the park, which we thought we might stop at if it didn't get too late or too cold, or if the babies weren't overtired. We might also swing by a friends' flat—friends with no kids—in which case we'd have to bring more toys, but we could leave the portacribs in the trunk for now.

♡ ♡ ♡ ♡ ♡ ♡ ♡ ♡ ♡ ♡ ♡ ♡ ♡ ♡ ♡ ♡ ♡

YOU KNOW YOU'RE A PARENT WHEN . . .

☼ you hum "Elmo's Song" all day at work

☼ bodily fluids of any kind no longer faze you

☼ you refer to your partner as "Mommy/Daddy"

☼ a station wagon, a house in the suburbs, and a better neighborhood suddenly make sense

☼ you start buying groceries and home sundries in bulk

☼ you've remembered how to do the "little teapot" dance

☼ you clap and say "Yay!" at the end of all musical refrains

☼ you decline a drink at a party because you have something to get home safe for

☼ it really does hurt you more than it hurts them

☼ you're sounding <u>exactly</u> like your parents

♡ ♡ ♡ ♡ ♡ ♡ ♡ ♡ ♡ ♡ ♡ ♡ ♡ ♡ ♡ ♡ ♡

As we battled squirming one-year-olds into strollers, placating them with rice cakes and coos, a young couple walked by. They were maybe five years younger than we were, or maybe they just looked that way. Their clothes were fashionable and unstained. They looked well rested. They looked as if they worked out. The woman wore the smallest of crocheted purses across her front. They walked by our sidewalk production and watched for a moment, and we watched them, much like the monkeys and the humans must stare at each other through the bars at a zoo. Only in this case, they were the humans and we were the other species (*parentis exhausteneous*). An exotic breed unfathomable to anyone not already a member of the tribe. They shook their heads in disbelief and moved on, leaving us to stare after them in chagrin. Each of us was thinking of a time, not so very long ago, when we were unfettered, young, and slim, with no more worries than at which restaurant to dine in the evening. Briefly it seemed that perhaps in having children we'd made a mistake. We could still be those people strolling the Marina on a perfect spring afternoon. We could still have easy, uncomplicated lives. We could fit into size 6 shorts—silk ones if we wanted! And our husbands would still have the energy to leap up and catch a Frisbee and have stomachs we could bounce quarters off.

Well. Revisionist history is all fine and good in some situations, but not in this case. Mostly because none of us could really conjure up what life was like before we had our children. What did we do with all that free time between dinner and bed, anyway? What exactly did we do on the weekends? None of us knew.

Fact was, we couldn't afford to waste time bemoaning the lifestyle we used to have. Life as we now knew it was tiring, but rich. In just one short year (the longest short year I ever lived through), we'd completely transformed ourselves into creatures we wouldn't have understood beforehand. We also knew that we couldn't go back to being that young couple strolling by. Even if something were to happen to our children, God forbid, we'd still be parents. We liked it here on Planet Parenthood, thank you, even if it did take a lot of extra work and the equipment was unwieldy. We also knew something the young couple didn't think we knew: they'd probably be joining us sooner or later.

And then they'd have to find their own damn parking spot.

READING FOR THE BLEARY-EYED

Right. As if you had any brain cells left. Presuming you can spare a few, there are many good books on parenting out there, but only a few great ones. Here is a short list of some greats every new parent should have lying around the house for inspiration, humor, advice, and information.

DR. SPOCK'S BABY AND CHILD CARE, Benjamin Spock, M.D., Michael B. Rothenberg, M.D. (Simon and Schuster, 7th edition, 1998). You need something by the bedside for those late-night mystery ailments. This is the book. Sure, your mother had a version, but this one is updated, so stop worrying.

DR. SPOCK ON PARENTING, Benjamin Spock, M.D. (Simon and Schuster, 1995). Again with the Spock. But I believe he's the most rational guy in the jungle of experts out there. His advice is solid, seasoned, and, I think, exactly on target.

EXPECTATIONS—30 WOMEN TALK ABOUT BECOMING A MOTHER, Laurie Wagner (Chronicle Books, 1998). A gorgeous and inspiring book of mothers on motherhood. Beautiful black and white photos by Anne Hamersky accompany each essay. Wagner lets her subjects—who range from teenage moms to suburban moms to reluctant moms—speak for themselves, and the result is powerful.

THE NEW FATHER: A DAD'S GUIDE TO THE FIRST YEAR, Armin A. Brott (Abbeville Press, 1997). Yeah, I know, it seems like everything is written with the new mom in mind, but stop pouting, here's something for you. Written by a man, for a man, with plenty of information on topics like sex and sporting events, which you won't be enjoying for a good long while.

OPERATING INSTRUCTIONS, Anne Lamott (Ballantine, 1993). Drop-dead accuracy on the host of new emotions you'll be up against as a parent, and screamingly funny (in parts) as well. More conservative types may be uncomfortable with her decidedly funky bent on some topics, but I have never read a more poignant, realistic book on what it's like to turn into a parent.

WHAT TO EXPECT THE FIRST YEAR, Arlene Eisenberg, Heidi E. Murkoff, and Sandee E. Hathaway (Workman Publishing, 1996). Like Eisenberg's *What to Expect When You're Expecting*, you pretty much have to have this at your bedside so you can read along and make sure your baby is doing what he's supposed to be doing.

INDEX

ABOUT THE AUTHOR

JULIE TILSNER has written for a number of national publications, including *Business Week* and the *New York Times*. She is a regular contributor to *Parenting Magazine* and Babycenter.com and writes a bi-monthly parenting column for *American Baby*. She lives in the San Francisco Bay Area with her husband and two small children and is starting to suspect the ghost of Erma Bombeck is living in her station wagon.

The baby book trusted by three generations of parents

THE BETTER HOMES AND GARDENS
NEW BABY BOOK

HUNDREDS OF AMERICA'S most respected baby experts have filled this book with the kind of sound professional help parents have relied on for more than forty years. Time-tested advice joins the latest findings of the American College of Obstetricians and Gynecologists to address all the questions and concerns of today's mothers and fathers. This NEW BABY BOOK is a complete, up-to-date, and reassuring reference for modern baby care.

- Care for mother and child during pregnancy
- Easing the discomforts of pregnancy, with new advice for mothers over 35
- Taking care of your child from infancy through six years
- Recent nutritional recommendations for the mother-to-be
- Help with breast-feeding and caring for the newborn
- Prenatal and postnatal exercises
- Choosing the proper day care

___26114-2 $7.50/$10.99 in Canada

NFB 33 9/01

Sound advice in these comprehensive maternity and childcare books from Bantam

- ❑ 24233-4 **THE FIRST TWELVE MONTHS OF LIFE: YOUR BABY'S GROWTH MONTH BY MONTH**

  Frank Caplan $6.99/$8.99

- ❑ 26438-9 **THE SECOND TWELVE MONTHS OF LIFE**

  Frank Caplan $6.99/$9.99

- ❑ 26967-4 **EARLY CHILDHOOD YEARS**

  Theresa Caplan $6.99/$8.50

- ❑ 58074-4 **THE COMPLETE BOOK OF BREASTFEEDING**—Marvin S. Eiger, M.D., and Sally Wendkos Olds $6.50/$9.99

- ❑ 37892-9 **FEEDING YOUR CHILD FOR LIFELONG HEALTH**

  —Susan B. Roberts, Ph.D. $15.95/$24.95

- ❑ 34632-6 **INFANT MASSAGE**

  Vimala Schneider McClure $14.95/$22.95

- ❑ 35339-X **YOUR CHILD'S HEALTH: A PEDIATRIC GUIDE FOR PARENTS**

  (Rev.—Barton D. Schmitt, M.D. $19.95/$29.95

- ❑ 58065-5 **BETTER HOMES AND GARDENS NEW BABY BOOK** (Revised) $7.50/$10.99

- ❑ 27145-8 **NAME YOUR BABY**—Lareina Rule $5.50/$8.50